CONTENTS

OPENING STATEMENT

S. HRG. 104–1

METHODS OF ESTIMATING THE IMPACT OF FEDERAL FISCAL POLICIES ON FEDERAL REVENUES

HEARING

BEFORE THE

COMMITTEE ON FINANCE
UNITED STATES SENATE

ONE HUNDRED FOURTH CONGRESS

FIRST SESSION

JANUARY 24, 1995

Printed for the use of the Committee on Finance

U.S. GOVERNMENT PRINTING OFFICE

88–270—CC WASHINGTON : 1995

For sale by the U.S. Government Printing Office
Superintendent of Documents, Congressional Sales Office, Washington, DC 20402
ISBN 0-16-046856-6

METHODS OF ESTIMATING THE IMPACT OF FEDERAL FISCAL POLICIES ON FEDERAL REVENUES

TUESDAY, JANUARY 24, 1995

U.S. SENATE,
COMMITTEE ON FINANCE,
Washington, DC.

The hearing was convened, pursuant to notice, at 9:30 a.m., in room SD–215, Dirksen Senate Office Building, Hon.

Bob Packwood (chairman of the committee) presiding.

Also present: Senators Moynihan, Baucus, Graham, Moseley-Braun, Chafee, Simpson, Pressler, D'Amato, Murkowski, and Nickles.

[The press release announcing the hearing follows:]

[Press Release No. 104–4, January 19, 1995]

FINANCE COMMITTEE SETS HEARING ON REVENUE ESTIMATING METHODS

WASHINGTON, DC.—Senator Bob Packwood (R-OR), Chairman of the Senate Committee on Finance, announced today that the Committee will conduct a hearing on the merits of static, behavioral, and dynamic methods of estimating the impact of federal fiscal policies on federal revenues.

The hearing will be held at *9:30 a.m., Tuesday, January 24, 1995,* in room SD–215 of the Dirksen Senate Office, Building.

"Revenue estimating methods have been a subject of considerable interest for those inside and outside government who follow the federal budget process closely. The purpose of this hearing will be educational in nature, providing Committee members an opportunity to hear from leading experts on this subject," Senator Packwood said.

OPENING STATEMENT OF HON. BOB PACKWOOD, A U.S. SENATOR FROM OREGON, CHAIRMAN, COMMITTEE ON FINANCE

The CHAIRMAN. Keeping in form with what Senator Moynihan did when he was Chairman, we are going to try to start these hearings on time whether or not other members are here. Others will be coming. I have indicated to them before, we will ask questions on a first-come, first-serve basis. Larry, you will be the second person to ask questions.

I have done the best I can in my past years as Chairman to discourage members from long opening statements. I am not going to make a long opening statement, other than to say, what the four of you have to present to us today may have as much effect on attempting to balance the budget—and I am assuming the Balanced Budget Amendment is going to pass—as anything else we might do.

You are familiar with the battle between dynamic, behavioral, and static scoring. It is easy enough, with some revenue estimates, to obviate your problems in the short run and aggravate them in the long run, but you can succeed in doing it.

Senator Pressler, do you have any opening statement?

Senator PRESSLER. I look forward to hearing the witnesses.

The CHAIRMAN. Then gentlemen, we will take you in the order that you are there, and we will start with Mr. Auerbach.

STATEMENT OF ALAN J. AUERBACH, ROBERT D. BURCH PROFESSOR OF TAX POLICY AND PUBLIC FINANCE, UNIVERSITY OF CALIFORNIA AT BERKELEY

Mr. AUERBACH. Thank you very much, Mr. Chairman. I am pleased to be here. I will give you a brief summary of my written testimony.

In the testimony I consider the current state of revenue estimation and, in particular, the feasibility and advisability of adopting changes to move to a scheme of so-called "dynamic" revenue estimation which would account for the net revenue changes resulting from macroeconomic policy.

I consider ways in which the revenue estimating process might be improved, and the role that revenue estimates should play in the policy process, a very central role at the moment.

Based on my reading of the evidence, I reach the following conclusions. First, in general, government revenue estimates have been very inaccurate during the past decade. Errors in predicting aggregate revenues and the components of aggregate revenues have been very large and forecasts have generally been overly optimistic. That is, typically actually revenue has fallen short of predictions.

To give you an example of that, on page 5 of my testimony there is a table which comes from a compilation of statistics from each year's budget, detailing forecast errors for each fiscal year by OMB, based on how revenues turned out compared to how they were originally forecast, and giving sources of error in the forecast, as a percentage of the total revenues for the period 1982–1993.

The things to focus on are sources of error that are macroeconomic and technical. Macroeconomic errors are due to overly optimistic predictions of macroeconomic performance which led to a shortfall of revenues. Technical errors are errors that remain after accounting for policy changes and macroeconomic changes.

If you take the macroeconomic and technical errors together you will see that the average error in the annual forecast of corporate income taxes was over 25 percent of corporate tax revenues. That is a 25 percent over-prediction of revenues; for excise taxes it was over 10 percent.

Mind you, these are short-term predictions, made just before the fiscal year started. If one looks at longer horizons, as I have done for CBO, the errors are larger, as one would expect.

These are large errors to explain. I believe that part of these errors are due to behavioral responses to taxation. In some preliminary work done in a paper I recently gave at the American Economic

Association meetings, I found that if one looks at policy changes and subsequent forecasting errors, there does seem to be a negative relationship.

That is, when revenues were predicted to go up as a result of policy changes, it turned out that revenue forecasts were too optimistic. More work has to be done on this, but I think this is something worth considering as the revenue estimating process is evaluated.

My third conclusion is that current budget rules need to be adjusted to reflect the forecasting difficulties that we have. The present mechanism by which apparently very precise revenue estimates are stuck into the budget calculation to see whether particular pieces of legislation pass muster does not really allow for the fact that, first predictions have been overly optimistic in the aggregate in the last several years and, second, there is a very large margin of error.

We are asking more of revenue estimators than we ask of meteorologists. Economists always like to compare themselves to meteorologists because they have an even worse forecasting record than we do. But we understand it in their case and we accept the fact that they are not sure whether it is going to rain tomorrow.

We would not want them to tell us that it will rain with certainty when there is really a 51 percent chance that it will rain. We like to know that there is uncertainty because it helps us make our plans. We should want to know that about revenue estimating as well.

Fourth, dynamic revenue estimating, in principle, is a good idea. After all, why not use all the information that we have? Why not take into account all the effects on revenue rather than just some? Why not look at the macroeconomic feedback effects?

That is true in principle, but I believe in practice, given the very much greater difficulties of making macroeconomic predictions of revenue effects that, given the pressure already on the revenue estimation process and the need for very precise estimates, it is probably an unworkable thing to try to do.

A lot of the fuel behind the demand for dynamic revenue estimation comes from the notion that it will, in general, make tax cuts look better. That is, it will make the revenue losses look smaller because of added growth.

An important point to make here is that not all tax cuts are going to increase growth, increase output, and, hence, increase revenue.

In our current economic environment, operating near full employment, tax cuts, which stimulate consumption, are not necessarily going to stimulate output. They may very well crowd out other forms of production such as investment. A reduction in investment is not going to stimulate growth, it's going to reduce growth.

So, if one were to venture to do a dynamic revenue estimate for a tax cut like that, it would probably go in the wrong direction for those who would like to see the tax cut cost less.

The final point that I would like to make is that, in spite of what I have said about the difficulty of making short-run forecasts, we should take long-run forecasts into greater consideration than we do right now.

The reconciliation of that statement with the fact that we have so much trouble estimating things in the short-run, is that the policy process now overstates the knowledge we have about the short-run by assuming that we have perfect knowledge. When we put 5-year budget forecasts into the budget process, there is no margin of error there. We assume that that is exactly what is going to happen and then we go about our business. Of anything after 5 years, we assume we have no knowledge at all because those things do not count in the budget process.

But we do have some information about the future. We do not have more information about the future than about the present, but we have some information and we should recognize that we have some information about the future and not as much information as we pretend to have about the present.

If we do that, then I think there will be less of a bias than there is right now toward measures which, either by design or by accident, have favorable revenue patterns in the short-run and very unfavorable revenue patterns in the long-run.

I am sad to say that some of the tax policies being suggested right now have this characteristic of looking very nice in the short-run and having very major deficit effects in the long-run.

In my own view, current fiscal policy is quite out of balance. We have significant long-run problems facing us.

And if we do not look at the long-run problems until we get there it is going to be far too late to deal with them adequately. Taking longer run projections into account in the revenue estimating process would help alleviate this problem.

Thank you.

The CHAIRMAN. I should have announced when Professor

Auerbach was testifying that he is the Robert Burch 1Professor of Tax Policy at the University of California at Berkeley and was previously the Deputy Chief of Staff of the Joint Tax Committee for a number of years. So he comes to this subject with a lot of knowledge.

[The prepared statement of Mr. Auerbach appears in the appendix.]

The CHAIRMAN. Our next witness is Dr. J.D. Foster, and he is the executive director and chief economist of the Tax Foundation in Washington, DC, and he used to work, both for Senator Simms and Senator Armstrong in the past.

Dr. Foster?

STATEMENT OF J.D. FOSTER, PH.D., EXECUTIVE DIRECTOR AND CHIEF ECONOMIST OF THE TAX FOUNDATION

Dr. FOSTER. Thank you, Mr. Chairman, members of the committee. It is nice to be back here again. I thank the committee for the opportunity to appear today. I commend the committee for meeting to debate what I would call nearly static versus dynamic revenue estimating, particularly when, really, there should not be a debate on this issue.

Accepting the limits of human knowledge, members should be able to take the accuracy of the revenue estimates for granted. But, instead, you have had to take for granted that the estimates have been occasionally, systematically, in error, as Dr. Auerbach's testimony attested.

Mr. Chairman, my written testimony gets into some of the issues surrounding dynamic scoring and I would like to restrict my oral remarks to a few disclaimers, a little overview, an example, and a couple of recommendations.

First, about the disclaimers. Given the rules under which they operate, the models the estimators use are extraordinarily complex instruments that have been developed over years and are based on some of the best data known to economists.

Second, the estimators are first-rate professionals who try to find the right answers, given the tools available.

Third, the estimators do not produce static estimates because they do take into account the most immediate response of taxpayers to a change in tax.

Fourth, dynamic revenue estimating is not, nor will it ever be, a magic wand capable of solving our fiscal problems. In most cases, even using dynamic scoring a "tax cut" will still reduce Federal receipts and a "tax increase" will still raise receipts.

The CHAIRMAN. Say that again.

Dr. FOSTER. Sir?

The CHAIRMAN. What you just said. Say that again.

Dr. FOSTER. I said, in most cases, even using dynamic scoring, a "tax cut" will still reduce Federal receipts.

The CHAIRMAN. All tax cuts.

Dr. FOSTER. In most cases. And tax increases will raise receipts in most cases.

Now, the Congress might be thought of as the captain of a great ship called the U.S.S. Federal Tax Policy, setting a destination as you sail the seven seas of alternative tax policies, and the revenue estimators are your navigators, providing course and speed to reach your destination.

Their charts and soundings are raw economic data, and their models are their compass, clocks, and sextant. Today the sextant cannot quite get the angles right, the compass shades a few degrees to the left, and the clock tends to run a little fast. So no matter how hard they try, using the tools they have at their disposal, your navigators cannot get you to your destination except by chance.

Now, the goal of revenue scoring is to produce the most accurate estimates possible so members can once again take the numbers for granted and focus on tax policy. The point is, dynamic scoring, done with appropriate care, can produce significantly more accurate estimates than are currently available. I think an example might bring this more into focus.

If you will recall, a 10 percent excise was levied in the 1990 Tax Bill on the value of personal boats and yachts that cost in excess of $100,000. This tax provides a good example of the distinction between nearly static and dynamic scoring, not because it was good or bad tax policy, nor because the estimates were better or worse than any other tax proposal, but because the enactment of the tax created a nice, well-defined event in tax policy.

Now, if 2,000 boats that cost an average of $150,000 would have otherwise been sold, a static estimate would indicate additional revenues of about $10 million.

The Joint Tax Committee assumed a reduction in the number of boats sold and produced a correspondingly smaller revenue estimate. They might have assumed, for example, that sales would decline by 5 percent, to 1,900 boats sold, and so reduce the revenue estimate to about $9.5 million.

The degree of demand response the Joint Tax Committee assumed can be, and was, questioned. But the first point is that they acknowledged the immediate market reaction to the tax and adjusted their revenue estimates of excise tax collections accordingly.

When they recognized that fewer boats would be sold, they also allowed that some boat builders would go out of business, that some workers would lose their jobs, and that suppliers to these former boat builders would lose some business as well. In the world of nearly static revenue estimating, these effects have no revenue consequences.

They assumed that all workers who once built boats immediately found employment at the same wages in other occupations, the capital previously employed in boat building was instantaneously reemployed doing something else, and that the former suppliers to the now defunct boat builders immediately began to supply the new businesses that sprang up.

In equilibrium, which is where economists usually are most comfortable, these assumptions were arguably appropriate. In application, these assumptions might have been reasonable, at least to a first approximation, in a 3- or 5- or 10-year time horizon, depending on the state of the national and local economies.

But to assume such a frictionless and immediate transition is simply unreasonable. The consequences for Federal receipts and outlays in the first years following the tax change were dramatic, I am sure.

Whatever receipts were estimated from the excise tax were initially offset by the loss of other receipts. When these businesses went under, they ceased paying income tax.

When the workers lost their jobs, they ceased paying income and payroll tax. In fact, their unemployment checks alone may have cost the government more revenue than was projected from the excise tax.

Therefore, to argue about whether or not the tax raised as much revenue as projected misses the point. We must look at tax proposals comprehensively, looking at the big picture.

Even if the luxury boat tax collected exactly the revenues projected, the other tax receipts that were lost and the additional expenditures that were incurred, all of which were ignored in the official estimates, conceivably cost the Treasury more than the tax itself brought in.

In conclusion, I would like to offer three simple recommendations. The first, is that the fullest possible range of feedback effects can and should be taken into account in estimating the change in revenues from a change in tax policy.

Second, everyone involved should recognize that we will not be able to switch over to dynamic scoring immediately.

This is a technology that will have to be mastered and applied where possible and where appropriate.

Finally, I believe the Congress should establish a working group, including representatives from the Joint Tax

Committee, CBO, Senate Finance Committee, House Ways and Means Committee, and a small number of outside experts to develop a business plan for moving to dynamic estimates.

Among other things, this working group will need to determine the principles to be used in dynamic analysis, a set of rules for determining when dynamic analysis should be used, a timetable for expanding the range of proposals qualifying for dynamic scoring, the additional staffing requirements needed, procedures for possibly publicizing the methods and assumptions the Joint Tax Committee uses, and, finally, the structure and responsibilities of an outside council of experts who will advise the Joint Tax

Committee in developing its dynamic models and to act as a sounding board and to provide quality control. Without such a working group it will be very difficult to assure that this new technology is implemented.

Looking down the road, many are predicting we will soon be looking at another tax reform. I remember, and I am sure the Chairman does far more clearly than I, how the revenue estimates at the time seemed to drive the debate.

No one knows what form tax reform will take, but it is certain we are likely to achieve the policy goals set if the revenue estimates are closer to the mark. This requires that we begin the transition to fully dynamic scoring today.

Thank you, sir.

The CHAIRMAN. Doctor, thank you.

[The prepared statement of Dr. Foster appears in the appendix.]

The CHAIRMAN. Next, we will take Glenn Hubbard, who is professor of finance and economics at Columbia University in New York, and was a former Deputy Assistant Secretary for Tax Analysis in the Treasury Department.

STATEMENT OF R. GLENN HUBBARD, RUSSELL L. CARSON PROFESSOR IN FINANCE AND ECONOMICS AT COLUMBIA UNIVERSITY

Mr. HUBBARD. Thank you, Mr. Chairman. I will reserve the lacuna of revenue estimates to the written testimony and focus my remarks on three areas: first, general issues in revenue estimating beyond the narrow point of macroeconomic feedback effects; second, concerns and issues with macro feedback effects; and then, finally, to give you a recommendation.

Before I talk about dynamic scoring or macro feedback effects, per se, I would like to spend a moment thinking about revenue estimation in the broader context of tax policy analysis.

When you debate proposals, you do so on two levels, discussing: first, the effect of proposals on the well-being of citizens, those currently here and those yet to come, and, second, budget rules that are used to determine short-term revenue impacts of "Revenue estimates" are forced to serve both of those masters in the current process.

I have a number of concerns with this current use of revenue estimates, and some of these reflect the concerns you have heard from Alan Auerbach and from J.D. Foster.

The first, is that a revenue estimate is just that—it is only an estimate. Each estimate that is prepared by the staff members of the JCT for the Congress or the Office of Tax Analysis in the administration reflects the best prediction of the effect of some proposal or some set of proposals on revenues over a period of time, say 5 years.

What economists do in these staffs in preparing these estimates for your use is to study available data and academic evidence, often under extreme time pressure.

The considerable uncertainty that goes into these point estimates of revenue effects that you receive suggest the usefulness of thinking about a range of revenue effects in forming your judgment about what the likely revenue consequences of a policy change are.

The second concern is to remember that assumptions matter. Economists live in worlds of assumptions, but often the world of revenue estimates makes the assumptions less clear than they might be. Let us suppose, for example, that we enter Nirvana for revenue estimators (and certainly for economics professors), and we could make estimates without statistical error.

We would still have a number of assumptions to bring to bear. If we have a tax increase to raise a given amount of revenue, how will those funds be used? To reduce other taxes? Increase spending? Is the change temporary or permanent? All of these questions shape the structure of a meaningful revenue estimate, and there is no one correct set or even convention of assumptions.

The third concern I have is that revenue estimates should inform you of the long-run consequences of policies under your consideration. By this, I mean that you need to be informed of the effect of a proposal on the present value of revenue to the government, or at least on revenue accruing over a suitably long period of time, such as the 10-year period required under Senate rules. That kind of information helps you to see long-term consequences without merely focusing on shorter-run timing effects.

A final general concern I want to raise is that any improvement or change you think about making to revenue estimating procedures needs to be coordinated with changes in distributional analysis of those same tax changes. Just as the information that is presented in revenue estimates should tell you about long-run consequences of proposals, distributional analysis should move beyond a 1-year or 5-year horizon. There is a lot of recent research by academic economists on measuring the lifetime burdens of tax policies and on examining the interagenerational transfers that accompany some major tax policies. I do not want to suggest to you that those studies or approaches are without their flaws, but I think that lengthening the horizon for distributional analysis, as you do for revenue analysis, gives you better information.

With these concerns in mind, I suggest that you initiate a review of current revenue estimating procedures. The bottom line of such a review could be the development of " revenue impact statement." In this revenue impact statement one could imagine, first, the conventional revenue estimate that is over some five-year or 10-year, depending on the rule, "budget window." Second, the statement should include a discussion of consequences of the proposal beyond those defined for the short run. Third, analysis of macro feedback effects, if any, and if significant, should be included and I will come back to that in a moment. Fourth, a discussion of broad efficiency or distributional effects of the proposal is important. Any decision you make regarding macroeconomic feedback effects should be part of that broader deliberation over budget procedures.

Now, let me discuss briefly the more narrow issue of "dynamic scoring" or macro feedback effects. As you know, in current practice for revenue estimating, either in the Congress or in the administration, revenue estimates do, indeed, attempt to predict many types of taxpayer responses to tax changes, in addition to estimating effects of the tax change on some initial tax base.

These predictions by the Joint Tax Committee staff and the Office of Tax Analysis staff make assumptions about behavioral responses—the " micro feedback effects," of the policy changes.

For example, the well-publicized difference in the revenue estimates prepared by the JCT and the Office of Tax Analysis for the capital gains proposals by the Bush Administration was a fight about "micro" feedback effects. In addition, though it is not often understood, some kinds of revenue estimates already incorporate macro feedback effects; the administration's budget receipts baseline already considers the collective effects of those proposals on economic activity in the forecast itself. So, in that sense, that collection of proposal already has the macro feedback effect.

Many have voiced concerns about macro feedback effects. Let me give you what, to me, are the compelling arguments for and against incorporating feedback effects, and leave you with a quick recommendation.

The two most significant arguments in favor of thinking about dynamic macro feedback effects for individual proposals are, first, that we believe that some tax policies do affect saving, investment, and economic growth. That is, presumably, one of the reasons we are thinking about those policy proposals. If we believe that, then a natural extension might be to "give credit" to the growth effects of those policies. A second argument in favor may be to help the enactment of growth-oriented or capital formation-oriented proposals.

At the same time, there are three arguments that suggest great caution. First, as I mentioned at the outset, economists' models are imprecise, far more imprecise than we may make them sound. This imprecision is only complicated by the incorporation of feedback effects. The second argument is that of economic risk. That is, if financial markets interpreted the switch as an attempt to abandon budget discipline, consequences of the shifts for interest rates could work in the opposite direction of the direct effect.

Third, the information requirements are substantial. From the administration's perspective, for each proposal for which this is done, the Council of Economic Advisers and the Office of Management and Budget would have to do a separate macroeconomic forecast—and that is not a number for GDP, it is a large set of variables—carry that to the

Treasury Department, which would then produce a new estimate. Over here, the Congressional Budget Office and the JCT would have to go through a similar exercise.

My suggestion to you, given these on the one hand/on the other hand concerns, is that you initiate a study of how and under what circumstances dynamic revenue estimates might be accomplished. In addition, I have some policy suggestions.

If you assemble staffs of the Office of Tax Analysis and the Joint Committee, along with some outside economists, to consider a small set of proposals, the range of answers you get on macro feedback effects, both within and across these groups, will give you some feel for whether this is a range of uncertainty with which you are comfortable. The proposals I would consider you to examine are ones that have been talked about a lot in this debate: a significant reduction in the capital gains tax rate, the enactment of a permanent investment tax credit, and a switch from income to consumption taxation. Those proposals span many of the big picture tax ideas and would serve as a useful framework for getting an answer.

To summarize, there are many, many problems in the current revenue estimating conventions. Frankly, dynamic revenue estimates would not be top of that list for me.

Such estimates do, however, address a very visible problem that has come to the attention of many policy makers, and I urge you to study those reforms with an eye toward designing informative revenue impact statements.

At the same time, I would urge you not to incorporate macro feedback effects in official revenue estimates, even for major policy proposals, prior to a general review of the estimating procedures more broadly.

Thank you.

The CHAIRMAN. Thank you.

[The prepared statement of Mr. Hubbard appears in the appendix.]

The CHAIRMAN. We will conclude with Mr. Niskanen, who is the President of the CATO Institute, and a long, longstanding Oregon native.

STATEMENT OF WILLIAM A. NISKANEN, CHAIRMAN, CATO INSTITUTE

Mr. NISKANEN. Thank you, Mr. Chairman and members of the committee. The role of numbers in policy analysis is to reduce the range of debate about whether to approve a specific policy change. That role will be served only if the process for estimating these numbers is not itself a matter of dispute.

The central point of my brief remarks is that any change in the process for estimating the revenue effects of tax changes should be broadly understood and approved, preferably by the key members of both parties in each House, and by the administration.

Such a change should be considered the equivalent of a change in the bylaws of a club, or a change in the scoring rules in an athletic league. Such changes should be approved only by the support of most of the affected groups, not by only those who expect to benefit most from the change in the short-run.

Some other considerations may help illustrate the issues bearing on this choice between static and dynamic revenue estimates. Static estimation is an application of arithmetic. Many politicians are not especially good at arithmetic, but it does not evoke much partisan dispute.

Dynamic estimating is based upon some model of economic behavior, a model that reflects some theory of how people behave, and estimates of how they respond to specific types of changes in the conditions they face. Some of the characteristic differences between parties involve differences on just these kinds of issues.

In that case, static estimation is somewhat like democracy: it may be the best deal we can make with our neighbors. But we should try to convince our neighbors if there is some reason to believe we can do better, and dynamic estimates can be much more accurate than static estimates.

In general, people will do more of some activity if the after-tax returns are increased and less of this activity if after-tax returns are reduced. That is the basis for the higher potential accuracy of the dynamic estimates. We would probably make better tax policy decisions, even on the basis of such a crude dynamic rule as assuming that tax increases increase revenue and that tax reductions reduce revenue by only half that estimated by static models.

But we should be able to do even better. There are still some differences in the estimates of the magnitude and timing of the responses to tax changes, but many of the differences in the numbers that you see can be resolved by focusing on the same scope of responses.

For prime age males, for example, the response of hours worked to changes in after-tax wages appears to be close to zero. The effect of taxes on taxable earnings, however, is a good bit higher, reflecting the response of taxable earnings to tax-induced effects on occupation, location, and tax avoidance. In technical terms, the elasticity of taxable earnings in response to tax changes is much higher than the elasticity of hours worked.

Similarly, the response to the savings rate to after—tax interest rates appears to be close to zero; the effect of tax rates on the taxable interest payments, however, is much higher, reflecting the tax-induced effect on the type of investments. Again, the elasticity of taxable income from capital is a good bit higher than the elasticity of the effect of taxes on savings behavior itself.

The full behavioral response to changes in taxes is often substantially higher than these first stage responses, especially in the long-run.

May I suggest, however, that the revenue estimators stop short of including the potential demand-side effects of tax changes? First, you should recognize that there continues to be a major disagreement among macro economists as to whether tax changes have a significant effect on aggregate demand.

On that issue, my own personal position is that most changes in fiscal policy, in general, have no significant effect on aggregate demand, but I acknowledge that many of my professional colleagues believe otherwise.

Second, any demand-side effects of tax changes can be offset by monetary policy. For these reasons, I suggest that estimates of the dynamic effects of tax changes on tax revenues should be based on supply-side models, not on the older form of Keynesian macromodels.

The next steps toward making sense of this issue, I suggest, are the following. First, it is important to put to rest the wholly false, albeit common, charge that the unexpected increases in the Federal deficit in the early 1980's were due to misleading dynamic supply-side revenue forecasts. In fact, all of the budget forecasts by both the administration and Congress were based on static revenue estimates; moreover, at the time in 1981, the OMB and CBO forecasts were very close.

The Federal deficits of the early 1980's proved to be substantially higher than any of us expected for several reasons: the unusually deep recession of 1981–1982, a faster-than-expected decline in inflation, and a failure by the Reagan Administration and Congress to maintain spending restraint beyond the first Reagan budget. All of the budget forecasts during this period substantially underestimated the deficit, but not because they were based upon dynamic or supply-side models.

Second, those who favor higher taxes should acknowledge that increases in the top marginal income tax rates generate little additional revenue; a given increase in tax rates at this level represents a larger proportionate reduction in the after-tax rate, and high income taxpayers have more opportunities for legal tax avoidance.

Similarly, those who favor lower taxes should acknowledge that some types of tax cuts reduce revenues by more than the static estimates. The $500 tax credit for children proposed in the House Republican contract, for example, would generate larger dynamic revenue losses to the extent that it increases the birth rate, or reduces participation of women in the paid labor force. These examples illustrate that dynamic revenue forecasts do not necessarily favor the preferred policy positions of either party.

Third, and this is quite important, the Joint Committee on Taxation should open up its estimating revenues and invite a broad peer review. May I suggest this process start by this committee asking the respected

National Bureau of Economic Research to sponsor some studies and then hold a conference on the JCT methodology and on the most important next steps to improve the forecasts. Leading public finance economists should be asked to comment on the JCT methodology and report to Congress, maybe at hearings before this committee, on their evaluations and their recommendations.

And finally, pending completion of this review of the

JCT methodology, my suggestion is that no change in this methodology at the moment is appropriate. A substantial consensus among leading public finance economists, I suggest, is probably necessary to broaden the support for proposed changes to this methodology across parties in Congress and with the administration.

And, as I suggested in introducing my remarks, more accurate revenue forecasts from the best possible dynamic models would help resolve differences in tax policy only if the methodology by which the forecast is generated is endorsed by most of the major participants in the policy debate.

Thank you.

[The prepared statement of Mr. Niskanen appears in the appendix.]

The CHAIRMAN. Mr. Niskanen, I might say, you are one of the few people I have heard testify accurately as to what the 1981 estimates were. Roughly, from February of 1980 until about mid-summer of 1981, we were all predicting huge surpluses by 1985; Joint Tax was, CBO was, OMB was. There was not much difference. They were all looking at $150–200 billion surpluses by 1985.

And, when Treasury testified as to their tax cuts, the overwhelming bulk of them were static revenues, dollar for dollar. President Reagan, I think probably correctly, thought if we did not give the money back, we would spend it. And had the money been there and we had not given it back, my hunch is we would have spent it. But there were static revenue declines based upon a percentage tax cut.

You mentioned excise taxes. Dr. Foster, I think it was you. And I am looking at the estimates. Actually, the boat tax collected slightly more in 1992 than we estimated. It was a small tax, anyway. But I look at these and wonder how we can be so far off. I will just go down the list. Airplanes. These are 1992 collections, but the estimate is what Joint Tax thought we would collect. They thought we would collect $4 million, we collected $400,000 on airplanes over $250,000. I mean, the figures are so small as to be irrelevant, but it's a negative 90 percent error.

You come down to the boats. Joint Tax estimated we would collect $9 million, we collected $12.4 million, or 33 percent plus. We collected more, but by the time you got down to the cost and the other effects of it we, in the net, lost money.

But then you get down to automobiles. We predicted in 1992 we would collect $69 million. We collected $296 million. We were off 400 percent. And you go down with furs, you go down with jewelry. The margins of error are extraordinary, sometimes up, sometimes down.

If that is the best we can do, how can we have any hope if we are going to consider consumption taxes, which are massive excise taxes, in essence, that we are anyplace close to what we are hoping the estimates might be?

Dr. FOSTER. Well, I think that is exactly the problem. In fact, as I understand it, for most excise tax changes, they use a simple rule of thumb and take the current predicted level of consumption of the product and apply the rule of thumb, a 25 percent reduction relative to the tax increase. They use that to adjust demand downward and then apply the tax rate to that level of consumption. I think, however, that——

The CHAIRMAN. But, I mean, how can we be so far off, sometimes up, sometimes down?

Dr. FOSTER. Well, I think what you have there is a good example of the limits of what we know in economics. They are off that much because product demand does things that they did not predict.

In some ways it is unfair to look at the revenue estimator's results in an after-the-fact fashion because the estimators take into account what they predict the economy is going to do, or what they predict the automobile market is going to do in the case of this excise, and they take their best guess.

88-270 - 95 - 2

Maybe they talk to GM and Toyota, and whomever, and they figure out what the market is going to do. Well, the market often does not do what they predict. If it did, GM and Toyota would tend to make money a lot more than they do. There is no way the Joint Tax Committee can predict better than General Motors can what the level of production of a certain type of automobile is going to be.

So, when you look after the fact, a lot of things have happened that the estimators could not have predicted having more to do with the underlying dynamics of the market than the effects of the tax itself.

I think the real problem with excise taxes though, is not just that they may be high or low on the actual collections from the excise, it is that whatever that projection is, they know, when you raise that tax, that there is going to be fewer units sold of whatever is being taxed. They know that means that there are going to be some businesses that are going to go out of business, some are going to be lost.

The CHAIRMAN. But this did not turn out to be true on cars. We sold more cars than we thought, despite the excise tax.

Dr. FOSTER. We sold more cars than we thought, but we probably, and almost certainly, sold fewer cars than we would have but for the tax. So even though more cars were sold, we would have sold even more if we had not raised the tax.

The CHAIRMAN. How do you know?

Dr. FOSTER. Well, that is the essence of what the price mechanism is all about. When the tax goes into effect, it raises the price of something. All we have to do is look at the Sunday supplements in our newspaper and see Giant Foods advertising 10 cent discounts on a tube of toothpaste to know that the market reacts to prices. That is the most fundamental aspect of economics—people respond to prices.

So, even if demand went up because of other factors, it would have gone up further but for the tax. That means that fewer workers were employed than would have been employed, and that means those people, for the period of their unemployment, are not paying income tax and they are not paying payroll tax. These effects are almost certainly greater than the excise tax collections that are recorded.

So, I think it is a matter of the forest versus the trees. The forest is the excise tax and the trees are all of the economic activity surrounding those trees.

Mr. NISKANEN. Mr. Chairman, in general, the short-run effects of a tax on long-lived capital assets will be larger than the long-term effects.

The CHAIRMAN. Now, say that again. The short-term effect——

Mr. NISKANEN. For capital items, for long-lived items, typically the short-run effects will be larger than——

The CHAIRMAN. Like cars?

Mr. NISKANEN. Yes. Well, typically for cars, but particularly for things like jewelry, yachts, and private airplanes.

The CHAIRMAN. The short-term effect would be what?

Mr. NISKANEN. Would be larger than the long-run effects. For short-lived items, normal consumer goods, the long-term effects are usually larger than the short-term effects.

The reason for it is that, for these long-lived items, you can change the timing of your purchases. The initial effects will defer purchases of jewelry and of private airplanes, yachts, and so forth, and even cars, as a rule.

A problem that I had when I was at Ford illustrates the problem that you face, in that when I first came there I would typically tell my superiors and colleagues that, at best, I can make a conditional forecast—an if, then, statement. If this happens, then that happens. And they said, Bill, that is not enough; we need a number for our planning process.

In many cases, economists are really not honest with you if they tell you a number by itself, because that number is a product of a set of assumptions. And you should at least be aware of the assumptions on which the number is generated because we cannot give you an unconditional number.

The CHAIRMAN. Thank you. We are going to hold ourselves to 5 minutes on questions on the first round. The order is Senators Pressler, Graham, Chafee, Simpson, D'Amato, Murkowski, Moseley-Braun, Baucus, and Moynihan.

And let me make one announcement about the meeting tomorrow. We will normally start our meetings at 9:30, but, to accommodate the House Banking Committee and Chairman Greenspan—he is going to testify there at 9:00 and will be over here at 10:00 in the morning—we will start at 10:00 tomorrow.

Senator Pressler?

Senator PRESSLER. Professor Martin Feldstein has been quoted as saying that "the existing static scoring models are based on the false assumption that taxes do not alter how much or how hard people work. Similarly, their calculations assume that taxes do not change how much people save. There is really no excuse for the tax analyst to ignore basic economic behavior that changes national economic outputs."

What is your response to that claim?

Mr. AUERBACH. I think there are a couple of things to clarify here. It may be that specific types of behavior are ignored. Indeed, in my own testimony I indicated, I think, that in the aggregate there may not have been enough allowance for behavioral effects in revenue estimates. We seem not to have picked that up as well as we should have.

But it is incorrect to say that, as a rule, all revenue estimates are static. We have been talking, for example, about excise taxes where a behavioral response is assumed.

It may be that for particular proposals, no labor supply effect is assumed.

That is, there are specific components of proposals for which a static assumption may be made, and it may be that that is what he is criticizing. I think that part of the problem is that, in many cases—and saving is a very good example, perhaps better than labor supply—there is such a range of predictions about what would happen if you lowered taxes on certain kinds of capital income, for example, that in order to produce any kind of a believable forecast, taking account of behavioral effects, one really would have to produce a range of estimates. As has been discussed here by the panel, the economic assumptions necessary to produce any particular estimate ought to be made clear.

There is a great range of beliefs about what taxes on saving would do to increase or decrease savings. A lot of it depends on how temporary or permanent it will be. I think he is right, in principle. We should certainly take account of behavioral effects wherever we can. But he does not tell us what the behavioral effects are, and many of us who have studied the problem for years do not know.

Senator PRESSLER. Well, I guess the State of California has adopted a more dynamic way of estimating State revenues. But how do you do that? Do you need a sociologist and a behavioral expert? In a lot of areas no previous data, or hard data exists, so you are just guessing.

Let me ask you, how great an impact would you expect dynamic scoring to have on interest rates and inflation?

Mr. NISKANEN. First approximation, zero, nothing. Inflation is dominantly a monetary phenomenon. Dynamic scoring of tax effects will not effect the major cause of inflation.

Senator PRESSLER. Considering the fact that responsiveness of taxes of a supply of capital from abroad is probably greater than the domestic savings elasticity, would you consider international capital flows to be a significant behavioral response? Are changes in the flow of international capital ever considered under the current revenue estimation method?

Dr. FOSTER. Senator, I do not believe that international capital flows are brought into account in the current estimation methods. I think the focus should not be so much on the specific effect of a tax change on international capital flows, but on the demand for capital stock in the U.S., and then we would look at that demand and compare that with what we expect the needed additional saving would be.

And the international capital flows meet that difference, so the focus probably ought to be on how the tax changes the economy's desired capital stock level relative to its current stock. Add into that equation how much we expect to save, and international capital flows make up the difference.

Mr. HUBBARD. If I could just add to that, international capital flows constitute a good example of behavioral effects considered under the current approach. They are an example of a response, a taxpayer response, albeit an international response. This is not really an example of the so called macroeconomic feedback effects.

Let me also say that we should get away from the use of the term "static." None of the contemporary revenue estimates is static; each has a wide range of what microeconomists would call elasticity or behavioral response effects, of which your point is an example.

Senator PRESSLER. Good.

Thank you very much, Mr. Chairman.

The CHAIRMAN. Senator Graham.

Senator GRAHAM. Thank you, Mr. Chairman.

Senator Pressler raised the California example of a revenue estimate that is reported to take greater advantage of behavioral responses.

If you were looking for a benchmark, what is the state of the art in revenue estimating, either among public agencies such as states or among private institutions, where would you go to find the best example of current revenue estimate? If this were the equivalent of an annual review of mutual fund managers and all revenue estimators were evaluated collectively, who would be at the top of the revenue estimating list?

Mr. AUERBACH. One of the problems in answering this question is that revenue estimation is unlike mutual fund performance evaluation or the comparison of macroeconomic forecasts, where we look and see how well different forecasters do, those are both types of forecasts where there is a lot of private interest.

It is in the interest of private businesses to know who the best interest rate forecaster is, who the best forecaster of GDP is, because it affects their business. So, there is a very competitive market in mutual fund performance evaluation and in forecasting of macroeconomic phenomena.

There is not the same kind of private market for revenue estimates. There is a private market, but it is inside the Beltway and as a result, there is not much comparison, public airing and study of the relative performance of different agencies.

We have little bits of knowledge and, as I think others on the panel have suggested, we need more information. I would not venture a guess at who is best right now. I do not think I have enough information. It has not been discussed and analyzed adequately in public.

Senator GRAHAM. I purposefully did not restrict my question to just public agencies. There are important economic decisions, maybe the most important economic decisions, that often depend on the assessment of what will be the reaction to various pricing changes.

An airline deciding to reduce its fares by 40 percent during the off season is just one example of where decisions on pricings are made, on the assumption that they will have behavioral reactions in the marketplace.

Again, my question is: Is there any place you would turn in the public or private sector that has had what would appear to be a superior record in terms of making those kinds of assessments and from whom we might learn something that would be relevant to the question of how the Federal Government might better estimate these responses in the marketplace?

Mr. HUBBARD. One place one might look is accounting firms, which often provide revenue estimate-like information to clients. As Alan Auerbach said, though, revenue estimates are not provided in a competitive marketplace. The one that counts is the one you take, irrespective of some judgments. There is not an easy benchmark to judge the right one.

Revenue estimators often do talk to industry experts, econometric modelers, and accounting firms in developing their own estimates. In that sense, then both the Joint Committee informing you, and the Office of Tax Analysis informing the administration, are trying to implement this sort of process. It is also not going to be easy for the outside academics that were mentioned by the panel today to come in and easily offer benchmarks, because offering such advice is not something that any of us do for a living.

Mr. NISKANEN. Senator Graham, they distinguish between the errors that are a consequence of macro errors—errors in forecasting macro conditions—and errors that are a consequence of bad revenue estimates given the macro conditions. Most of the errors in the revenue forecast that we have observed have been a consequence of errors in the macro forecast.

Nobody has a consistently very good track record on macro forecasts. There are some rankings. The CBO forecasts over the past 15 years have been slightly better than the administrations of either party over that period of time. The blue chip forecasts are about as good as any, but there are relatively few people who can do consistently better than the blue chip forecasts, or the CBO forecasts, over the same period of time.

On the revenue estimates themselves, my own judgment is that the best available model is the TAXSIM model developed at the National Bureau of Economic Research. That is a model in which the structure of the model and the co-efficients that go into it are subject to substantial peer review among the best public finance economists in the country.

If you were to adopt wholesale an outside model, I think that is where you would start, although I think the best way to start is a very careful peer review of the JCT methodology itself, based upon the evaluation by leading outside people.

Senator GRAHAM. Thank you, Mr. Chairman.

The CHAIRMAN. Senator Chafee.

Senator CHAFEE. Thank you, Mr. Chairman.

I must say, Mr. Chairman, I found this somewhat complicated. And if somebody asks me what a macro feedback effect is, I would ask you, Mr. Chairman, to explain it, while I run out to an appointment. [Laughter.]

Let us take you, Mr. Auerbach, whom we have seen here frequently. What exactly are you saying? [Laughter.]

I notice on page 8 of your testimony that you asked the question, "Should dynamic revenue scoring be used?" And you say the most serious problem in your application of dynamic revenue estimation is the uncertainty surrounding estimates. I think we would all agree with you on that. What do you recommend, briefly?

Mr. AUERBACH. Well, I have to say, on the one hand, on the other hand. I recommend that in the current environment, given the fact that the budget process does not adequately take account of uncertainty and requires a specific number, and given the pressure that estimators are already under to deliver estimates quickly that have a great deal of importance, that this is not the time, if there ever is a time, to incorporate dynamic feedback effects, because dynamic feedback effects——

Senator CHAFEE. Does dynamic feedback effects mean dynamic scoring?

Mr. AUERBACH. Yes. That is, we know that there will be macroeconomic changes. CBO and OMB forecasts change every quarter and they take account of predicted changes in macroeconomic behavior on revenues. What they do not do is trace those changes to tax policies.

They do not say, unemployment is going to be down beyond what we thought, or GDP is going to be above what we thought, because of this or that policy—making that additional connection and putting it back into the revenue estimate and saying, unemployment is going to be lower, therefore, income is going to be higher, therefore, revenue is going to be higher, therefore, we should deduct that additional revenue from the tax cut we just introduced. That is a macroeconomic feedback effect, dynamic scoring, if you like.

It would be wonderful if we had any idea what those numbers were. It is much more difficult than most people realize to make the predictions that are being made. The Chairman's example of the luxury tax performance is an illustration of that. In trying to go to another level of prediction and say, well, what is——

Senator CHAFEE. But you are saying static. I presume that these figures that the Chairman gave us were static estimates.

Mr. AUERBACH. Well, not static. They incorporate behavioral effects in the affected industries.

Senator CHAFEE. I see. But did not go beyond that.

Mr. AUERBACH. That is right.

Senator CHAFEE. And you are saying, it is hard enough to do that, as indicated by their being 400 percent off.

Mr. AUERBACH. Right.

Senator CHAFEE. And so do not get into trying to go beyond that.

Mr. AUERBACH. In principle, it is a wonderful idea. As scientists, economists say, the more information the better; let us use all the information we have. If it were being given to Congress for informational purposes only, do not use without additional advice, that would be fine, but that is not how revenue estimates are produced and used in the policy process.

It would be very unfortunate to get what would essentially be an educated guess by a revenue estimator under severe time pressure and great informational constraints and have that be what drives tax policy.

Senator CHAFEE. All right. What do you say to that, Dr. Foster, do you agree?

Dr. FOSTER. With some of it. What I would say is, there is an old saying, the best is the enemy of the good.

We know that our current estimates are frequently, as we have heard here, very far off. We know that there are things that the estimation process does not take into account that we do know something about. We may not know everything there is to know about it, we may not have the most precise figure and estimate of response that we would like, but we have ranges.

By our research on a wide variety of things that we have studied for a long time, we do have ranges of how people are going to be responding to a change in a price, as induced by a tax. So we know we have this range. We can certainly take the low end, the most conservative element of that range, and end up with an estimate that is more precise than what we have now.

Now we assume that figure is zero, which is absurd, particularly in light of the fact that we know something about what that range of response is going to be; we know something about how people

88-270 - 95 - 3

will respond, we know something of what happens when people lose their jobs and stop paying income tax, and we ought to take that into account.

We certainly are going to have to do it with some care and caution, and this is not going to happen all at once, but it is something we should get on to. My point is simply this, it can be done, and we ought to get about the business of doing it.

Senator CHAFEE. Well, I must say, on the boat thing, it did not take a Phi Beta Kappa to understand what was going to happen there.

There is only one other thing I would like to say. On the spending side, we do not get into dynamic scoring. In other words, if you spend money on education, you are going to have increased tax revenue because these people are going to get better jobs, and so forth, and so on.

This has all been very clear, Mr. Chairman. I appreciate the opportunity to ask questions.

Senator MOYNIHAN. Your questions have been clarifying.

Senator CHAFEE. Yes. Thank you very much.

The CHAIRMAN. Senator Moseley-Braun.

Senator MOSELEY-BRAUN. Thank you very much, Mr. Chairman

In the first instance with regard to the testimony I have heard so far, I have really been struck by the kind of assumption—actually it was stated in one of the presentations—that politicians do not count very well, and that, in other testimony, Congress has less interest in accurate forecasts than, for example, a mutual fund manager might have with regard to investors' money.

If anything, I would point out that that is why we are here today listening to this. I mean, we are faced right now with trying to address budget deficit issues, we are trying to address the issue of fiscal integrity, particularly going into this next century, and what it is going to mean in terms of the capacity of our government to function in the public interest; we are facing even unfunded mandates, which is the legislation, as you know, that is on the floor now. So we are trying, I think, to get some hold, get some fix on this very complicated process and to get the best that the best and brightest minds have to offer.

So, at the outset, I would just want to caution that, because I think it gives the wrong impression to suggest that we are more profligate with taxpayer money than a mutual fund manager might be with investor money. We are actually trying to get a fix so we do not run into the errors that estimation has given rise to in the past.

Having said that, I want to go back to Senator Graham's question, because I think it was a very good question. He asked you—and I can see all of you as professionals in the field kind of being put on the spot with his question—who has done the best job, who, over time?

Who is generally more accurate? That is not to say that any one predictor or any one group of analysts will always do a better job, but in the main, where can we look for the better figures?

Now, we have documents here of CBO being off on its forecast, and that is not to say they are not good people at CBO and that is not to say that they are not trying, but the fact is, since 1980, they have been off most of the time. In fact, if anything, they have been more conservative than not.

So, assuming for a moment that CBO comes in on the conservative end and Treasury estimates are off also, and then we have the Joint Taxation Committee, would you, therefore, suggest that what we need to do really is expand the universe of our examination and look to some of these private reports and look to the private sector and private groups?

So, two questions. Senator Graham's, I want to pick up and ask somebody to give us a straight answer to his question, and then the second question is, would you suggest expanding the range of our inquiry so that we can come up with a better mix of estimations?

Mr. HUBBARD. I would like to attempt a straight answer—as straight, at least, as an economist's answer is likely to be. There are two problems here. One, is the macroeconomic errors. That is, we are wrong because we do not know whether the economy will be growing fast, growing slowly, or not at all.

Second, are microeconomic errors. That is, we are uncertain about how taxpayers will respond to policy changes. There are different organizations that make a living trying to second-guess those two types of errors. For example there are a number of econometric forecasting firms that sell forecasts of the economy, the blue chip index sort of summarizes those and gives a consensus forecast. At the level of micro forecasts, however, the place to look would be the analyses of the industries most affected; they have the market incentives to try to get it right. As I mentioned earlier in responding to Senator Graham's question, revenue estimators do try to look at those micro forecasts.

I think one does want to include the private sector in the forecasting process—not necessarily cherry-picking revenue estimates from the forecaster of the month, but including all the information available in trying to get at the best forecast.

I believe what Alan Auerbach hinted at in the value of competition in the case of mutual funds was not at all that members do not care about the budgeting process, but merely, that you do not have the range of choice that the private sector has. There is a certain discipline process in stock market forecasting or asset market forecasting. Namely, if a forecaster gets it wrong too many times, nobody buys his or her services anymore and you do not know about him or her.

Senator MOSELEY-BRAUN. We have the same problem. But go ahead.

Mr. HUBBARD. But you have monopolists providing your revenue estimates, so it is not quite the same thing. I think that was what was meant.

Senator MOSELEY-BRAUN. You mean lifetime civil servants providing our revenue estimates as opposed to people who have to stand for election. Is that what you are suggesting?

Mr. HUBBARD. You do not have a competitive process of providing revenue estimates.

Senator MOSELEY-BRAUN. Mr. Auerbach?

Mr. AUERBACH. Well, that does clarify the problem. I certainly was not suggesting any profligacy on the part of legislators. Simply that the market mechanism is a wonderful thing, it disciplines suppliers without anybody trying to do it.

And there is an unfortunate kind of competitive revenue estimating that goes on in Washington, but it is not to get the most accurate forecasts, it is to get forecasts that lead to one legislative outcome or another, and that is not the kind of information that helps you. You want accuracy, you do not want biased estimates.

Senator MOSELEY-BRAUN. We want good numbers. Right.

Mr. AUERBACH. And, unfortunately, the market is providing self-interested estimates. The private sector inside the Beltway is providing you with self-interested estimates, not with estimates that seek to achieve accuracy.

The CHAIRMAN. Go ahead.

Senator MOSELEY-BRAUN. Well, in getting to the second question, particularly now with the information explosion in computers and all of the technology that we have to get basic microeconomic on the one hand, and macroeconomic on the other, data into the mix for purposes of forecasting, would you have any recommendation about where we would best look, or is it just back to the suggestion that you made that we ought to just continue to study this for awhile before we do anything?

Mr. NISKANEN. Senator, I suggest you have no real alternative but to rely on the JCT for most of the estimates that are made, and the challenge is to improve the JCT methodology. I think that that can be done by opening up that methodology for an extensive peer review and then having maybe a periodic review of the JCT methodology and their coefficients by an outside group.

Now, when there is controversy, you will hear about it because there are people who have a stake in the way the numbers come out. You will hear about it. You do not need to worry about hearing about whether people believe that JCT numbers are wrong. I think you have reason to worry whether they are the best available.

On this prior question of how much of the macro effects should be taken into account, again, I do not think it is administratively possible to generate the macro effects of every proposed policy change.

The way the process works is that, for a period of time, you are working with a given set of macro forecasts and then within those forecasts the JCT and other bodies can rather quickly give you estimates of the effects of specific policy changes. But they cannot change the macro forecast every time they are evaluating a specific policy change.

The macro forecast is based, presumably, in the administration and in Congress, on the set of policy changes they expect during that period of time, but cannot realistically and administratively reflect the effects of the particular change that you have asked them to evaluate.

Senator MOSELEY-BRAUN. Thank you, Mr. Chairman.

The CHAIRMAN. Senator Moynihan.

Senator MOYNIHAN. I would carry on, if I might, Mr. Chairman with Senator Moseley-Braun's questions, and just ask for some advice from the panel more than anything else.

Galbraith, in one of his antic moments, described economics as a failed profession. Dr. Niskanen said, nobody has a consistently good record on estimates, and Dr. Auerbach says, it's not a science.

I just wondered what your advice would be from the point of view of the profession. I am now in my 19th year on the Finance Committee. When we began, when I first came here, the finances of the American Government were solid. We had continued our concerns with unemployment at levels which reflected, really, the aftermath of the Great Depression and the Keynesian era.

But there was no debt of any consequence and there was no crisis of any importance at the level of public finance, yet, the prestige of economics was never greater and schools of economics were very competitive.

And 19 years later we are immobilized by debt and incapable of most actions because,as regards any issue of public policy, the first question asked about it is, how much will it cost, and the answer is, you cannot afford it.

This came about somehow. If I can say, Dr. Niskanen, I recognize your point about the forecasts in 1981. The Chairman has frequently made that point of anticipation of the continuation of inflation and not seeing a sharp crash. It looked like the budget was in balance indefinitely.

But here we are. Ought we scale back our dependence on this kind of analysis on the grounds that it gives a level of confidence that is not warranted? You are senior, sir. Why do you not speak first? I am sure you have made more mistakes than anybody else.

Mr. NISKANEN. Yes. I have had longer time to make mistakes than my colleagues. I think economists in the 1960's and maybe early 1970's promised far too much. The comeuppance was the failure to explain what came to be called stagflation, a combination of high inflation and high unemployment, and that broke open what was a Keynesian lock on the general perspectives on economics.

Senator MOYNIHAN. When Arthur Burns said, things do not work the way they used to.

Mr. NISKANEN. That is right. Nixon was the last president to say, "I am a Keynesian." That was about the end of Keynesian dominance over macro policy.

Part of our problem, I think, is that, like many people, we are not sufficiently humble, but we have been humbled. We have been much more humble in the recent 15 years than in the prior period of time.

Part of it is that people do not listen to our conditions. In other words, at best we can make if, then statements; if this happens, then this is likely to happen with a certain probability. And what the audience often forgets is what the if is, and what the probability is. Complex planning processes need a number, and the if and the probability gets dropped in that business. I think that is a good bit of why we often oversimplify it, is because our audience wants us to oversimplify it.

My profession has been relatively immune from a situation of using our techniques to justify any conceivable position. Most economists are really not for sale to the highest bidder because our peer group is our fellow professionals and that is the group whom we are seeing approval of, as a rule.

That is an enormously valuable discipline to you and that will give you more honest advice, typically, than you will get from what Mr. Galbraith inappropriately called, as salesmen.

Senator MOYNIHAN. Did he do that? I think he just said that it was a failed profession.

Mr. HUBBARD. I would like to pick up on the "if, then" comment. There are two issues in revenue estimates, assumptions and analysis. When we criticize estimates or pick apart numbers, as the Chairman was doing in his example, one has to sort out analytical failure from failed assumptions. Often, we do not make clear what assumptions are in an analysis. Your output is "a number."

Senator MOYNIHAN. Then it concretizes a very complex issue.

Mr. HUBBARD. If you ask questions of the JCT staff, they will no doubt walk through the analysis with you, but less so the assumptions. I think what you need is something along the lines of the revenue impact statement I suggested, some broader statement of revenue consequences. The problem with that, of course, is it does not fit nicely in the budget scoring rules. This is really an issue far broader than just scoring.

Senator MOYNIHAN. Mr. Chairman, my time is up. Can I just suggest to Dr. Foster and Dr. Auerbach, that we could usefully be tutored in how to be careful with what you can produce. As you are more careful, you are necessarily more complex, which makes you more distant from us.

I mean, I can remember a time in the Kennedy White House when the Secretary of Labor would take you over to lunch. And they would stop at the table, the Chairman of the Council of Economic Advisors, and he would look at his watch and say, well, now, it has been 1 month, 29 days since we sent up that tax bill and since you haven't passed it, the cost to GNP has been $138,400,000. Well, we know you do not know that.

But, as you learn what you do not know, of necessity your message becomes more complex and, therefore, more difficult for us to absorb. I just put it out for a subject for the profession because we do not have a lot to show for the last 15 years. I mean, obviously things have gone wrong which have produced a kind of crisis of the republic. It cannot govern for lack of resources, which is what economics is all about.

Mr. NISKANEN. Senator Moynihan, I think that there are some very important lessons in the past 15 years that we have learned more generally. One, is that inflation is dominantly a monetary phenomenon.

The CHAIRMAN. Inflation is what?

Mr. NISKANEN. Dominantly a monetary phenomenon. In 1981, the major critics of the Reagan budget believed that it would be wildly inflationary. Most of the critics in the spring of 1981, in testimony before this and other committees, said the Reagan budget would be wildly inflationary. As it turned out, inflation came down faster than the optimists anticipated.

Senator MOYNIHAN. Which is what happened to our revenue estimates.

Mr. NISKANEN. That is right. That is what happened to the revenue estimates.

Second, I think that we have learned that the conjecture by Mr. Barro that he attributes to Mr. Ricardo is probably wrong, that deficits have no effect on savings because they are offset by a corresponding increase in private savings.

What we found during the 1980's is that we had both a substantial increase in deficits and a dramatic and disturbing fall in private savings.

Senator MOYNIHAN. Which is a problem that you might compare to stagflation.

Mr. NISKANEN. Yes.

Senator MOYNIHAN. This was not supposed to happen, and we cannot explain that.

Mr. NISKANEN. Right. And I think that we should learn from that experience. The 1980's were an interesting period, generally a quite productive period, and we should learn from them.

Senator MOYNIHAN. Thank you very much.

Thank you, Mr. Chairman.

The CHAIRMAN. For the audience, I might expand on Mr. Niskanen's comment about inflation, and Senator Moynihan's. We used to be able to figure, before we indexed the Tax Code, that for each 1 percent of inflation revenues would grow, on average, about 1.7 percent.

In 1981, we were still in the third or fourth year of 12, 13, 14 percent of inflation and we were projecting that to continue and the revenues were going to roll in beyond imagination. First, the inflation just fell dramatically and revenues fell. Then nobody predicted the recession, and they fell further. It was nobody's fault; nobody was predicting it.

I want to shift the subject. You mention that there was no crisis. It is all relative. Just before you came, Pat, or two or 3 years before you came, we thought Federal spending was so bad that we considered, and the House passed, a bill delegating to President Nixon the power to cut the budget where he wanted—we exempted the usual suspects, like Social Security—when it exceeded $250 billion. I do not mean deficit, I mean budget.

Today the deficits are bigger than the budget. But that is how bad we thought the crisis was. And that passed the House, Wilbur Mills championing it, and died in the Senate on a close vote. But we had great debates about power and the right of the purse, and should we make those kind of delegations.

I want to shift over to the savings and investment subject because we are going to be into this all year long. Let me give you a couple of statements, and you tell me if my facts are right.

As a rule of thumb, the major industrial countries, the older industrial countries that we compete with, tax anyplace from 10–25 percent more of their gross domestic product than we do in terms of total taxation. We are around 35 percent of many of the European countries, around 45–50 percent, to some of the Scandinavian countries in excess of 60 percent. Is that roughly accurate?

Mr. AUERBACH. Yes, sir.

Dr. FOSTER. Yes, sir.

The CHAIRMAN. And of their total taxes—and this is where I want to distinguish it carefully—a higher percentage of it comes from consumption than this country and a lower percentage of it comes from capital and investment, although in total it may be greater because they tax more. But the percentage of the mix tilts more toward consumption than ours does. Is that correct?

Mr. NISKANEN. Yes.

Dr. FOSTER. Yes.

The CHAIRMAN. Third, of the newer countries that we are competing with, the Indonesias, the Malaysias, the Singapores, the Koreas, the Taiwans, they are more inclined to have a total tax rate of around 19, 20, 21, 22 percent of their gross domestic product rather than our 35 percent, or rather than our older industrial competitors, 45–60 percent. Now, I have checked those figures and I think they are right.

So my first question is, absent the mix of how much consumption versus how much savings on capital and income, absent the mix, is a country with a lower—and I do not mean a country so undeveloped it is almost a moot point; these countries I mentioned are not really undeveloped, they're coming right along—level of total taxation likely to make you a more effective competitor in the world, or is it not particularly a factor? I will start with Dr. Auerbach.

Mr. AUERBACH. I do not think you can answer the question on the basis of that information alone. It depends on what you are spending the money on. If you are spending the money on infrastructure, educational system, and so forth, it is quite different than if you are spending it on transfer payments, whereas, we are spending a rapidly increasing share of our budget on transfer payments.

Presumably, when a country develops and it becomes wealthier and can afford to purchase infrastructure and things like that, this makes it more productive. It is probably an easier question if you are looking, perhaps, at the Nordic countries. You mentioned very high tax rates, where they have a very significant problem with transfers being a large part of their budgets, and the effects that that has.

The CHAIRMAN. They are almost uncompetitive in the world economy now, with a few maybe specialty exceptions.

Mr. AUERBACH. I think they recognize that, although they are having a lot of difficulty doing anything about it, as we can understand.

The CHAIRMAN. Once you pass a law giving a transfer payment, it is almost like it came with Moses. It is difficult to undo it.

Dr. Foster, do you have a comment on my question?

Dr. FOSTER. Yes. Just one caveat with regard to the numbers themselves. As you know, in Europe a lot of the health care is financed through the government, so you have health care included in that mix. You have to decide to either subtract it out, or add it in on the U.S. side to have comparables.

Dr. Auerbach put his finger right on the point. It is not so much the level of taxation as it is the level of spending, and, secondarily, what you spend it on because your comparison then is between infrastructure versus entitlements versus private use of the resources. So, that is really where your focus should be. And, having determined the level of spending, then the level of taxation follows.

The CHAIRMAN. Mr. Hubbard?

Mr. HUBBARD. Yes. The key initial point is that saving and capital accumulation are too low in the United States. There is, however, more at work in this problem than just capital income taxation. It is not just the fact that we have higher capital taxes than some other countries that accounts for the problem. Other intergenerational redistribution issues and social insurance issues that may be more important.

I think Alan Auerbach hit on the central point for you, which regards benefit taxation. Think about two local communities: If one has a higher tax rate than the other, it may also be providing a higher level of services. So, you really have to look at both the level of spending and the allocation of spending.

The CHAIRMAN. Mr. Niskanen.

Mr. NISKANEN. There is an important new study by the National Bureau on just this issue about the effect of the level and structure of taxes on international competitiveness. They find surprisingly big effects.

The CHAIRMAN. On the total level of taxation?

Mr. NISKANEN. The effect of marginal tax rates on real unit labor costs. And I will have to review that study in detail, but it may be valuable for the JTC or your committee to review this study at some future time. It has quite dramatic results.

The CHAIRMAN. Senator Moseley-Braun.

Senator MOSELEY-BRAUN. Thank you very much, Mr.

Chairman I will not be long, except to say that I certainly hope that we can have a report, if not a hearing, of this committee, Mr. Chairman, but that the professionals will have the opportunity for some peer review in terms of looking at what the budget scoring rules are, what the fundamental assumptions are, what goes into the mix, and the methodologies and the processes even for making these estimates, because we really do need to have numbers.

Assuming for a moment that this is an art and not yet a science, we do need to have better numbers so that we can have some reasonable expectation that we could make rational predictions and rational policy decisions.

Or, alternatively, then maybe the answer, Senator Moynihan, as you suggested, is to go back to the old rule of thumb, your gut kind of reaction, and not worry about the numbers and just make decisions based on what feels right to do.

It seems to me that in these times we ought to be able to have more reliance on the numbers than on the economic forecast, because so much depends on decisions about whether or not we invest in education and infrastructure development or just give people a tax cut and expect them to do it. Those kinds of decisions will hinge on the results of what you do.

So, I want to just encourage a continuous discussion within the profession and within the Joint Committee and the CBO, and the people who are the experts in this area, to take a look at some of the fundamentals and perhaps report back to us so that we can continue this discussion based on the results of your examination.

Thank you, Mr. Chairman.

Senator MOYNIHAN. Can I ask a question?

The CHAIRMAN. Yes, by all means.

88-270 - 95 - 4

Senator MOYNIHAN. To follow Senator Moseley-Braun, it was a measure of some urgency because if we look at all the complexities we encounter, there are some successes, some failures. But that long building up of a crisis to which I have referred, in the early 1970's, the Chairman mentioned the feeling that we ought to give the President the power of impoundment, and then we got mad about that as we got mad about Jefferson and those gun boats on the Mississippi. The next thing you know, we had the Budget Act, and all that. But now, instead of just the Budget Act, we are going to change the constitution. That is what we are proposing to do, it appears to be two-thirds of both bodies are of the view that we ought. That is a big proposition.

I mean, I can recall a time not that distant when it was felt that the problem of Federal Government was that Congress would not spend enough money; the problem of our economy, a dread affliction called fiscal drag.

Under President Nixon, George Schultz would prepare a budget, a full employment budget, in which outlays would equal the capacity of the economy—revenues from a full employment economy. You build a deficit into the budget so that you would stimulate up, and you had a problem of not spending enough money.

Now, we have told ourselves that there is something innate in a democratic polity such that it cannot be trusted to manage its fiscal affairs, and the constitution has to be amended and put us on an agricultural cycle, 12 months, and require that this be done.

Mr. Chairman, could I poll the panel? Do you suppose that a constitutional amendment could be made to work without reference to external parties, as for example the Supreme Court, to decide whether we stop the clock at December 31st, it is now March 12th, and we cannot do it, et cetera, and so forth. I mean, how do you all feel about this?

Mr. NISKANEN. Senator Moynihan, the amendment that is before Congress requires a super majority vote to approve a budget with a deficit in it. It does not require an actual balance. In other words, it is a vote on the Congressional Budget Resolution, in effect, and it would permit all of the automatic stabilizers to continue to operate.

In other words, if economic conditions are stronger than expected there will be a surplus; in that case, weaker than expected, there will be a deficit. It does not prohibit a deficit on, as you say, an agricultural cycle, or require a balance on that cycle.

The case, I think, for the two main provisions of the amendment is quite different. One, the case for the Balanced Budget provision is that our children and their children are not very well-represented in this body.

Senator MOYNIHAN. Nor ever have been.

Mr. NISKANEN. Nor ever have been. Second, the case for some kind of stronger tax provision is a consequence of the fact that the enumerated powers no longer bind the scope of the Federal fiscal reach, and have not for 60 years.

We operated, for the first 140 years of our history, by basically two rules. In other words, the Federal Government did little more than the enumerated powers, and second is, we operated by a rule that the Federal Government would borrow only during recessions and wars.

Those two rules have broken down, and that is the reason why we need a new rule. I think it can be kept out of the courts. It is important to recognize that it does not prescribe outcomes, it prescribes rules and the rules are on the budget ex ante and not on fiscal outcomes ex poste. So, I think it can be done.

Now, whether it is good policy will be your decision and not mine, but I support the measures that are before Congress.

Senator MOYNIHAN. Dr. Hubbard?

Mr. HUBBARD. I think whether a Balanced Budget Amendment is a good idea depends on what the question is. I take the central concern to be the level and allocation of spending, which requires making some very difficult policy choices. There are many differences of opinion over those choices. There is a chance that the Balanced Budget Amendment, writ large and the specific one before the Congress, can trivialize those difficult choices. There are also a number of technical problems, but I think the central issue is deciding what the question is.

Senator MOYNIHAN. Dr. Foster?

Dr. FOSTER. I definitely would agree that the central issue is deciding what the question is. In a ranking of all the possible things to worry about, the level of spending would bother me more than a deficit in a given year.

But I think the choice in considering the Balanced Budget Amendment is not really whether we should have the amendment or not, the question properly framed is, should we have the amendment or should we continue with the status quo with the rules that have been broken and the deficits that have gone on for a number of years now and are projected to continue?

I would suggest that the evidence suggests that we have got to have the amendment. Whatever down sides there may be to that, we simply cannot continue with the current procedures and patterns in deficit spending forever. If there are consequences for that for the level of spending, so much the better.

Senator MOYNIHAN. Mr. Chairman, could we just ask Dr. Auerbach?

The CHAIRMAN. Go right ahead.

Senator MOYNIHAN. Dr. Auerbach.

Mr. AUERBACH. Yes. I think there are two very major problems with the Balanced Budget Amendment. First of all, we have been here talking for an hour and a half about revenue estimates. And one of the things we have learned of the budget rules since 1985 is that having rules that apply prospectively, and just letting bygones be bygones after it turns out we did not do very well in our estimate, is not particularly a good idea because there is no correction mechanism for the mistakes that we make.

Second, we should be very concerned about our young and future generations because there is going to be a real problem in the next century, given the path that we are on. But controlling the deficit does not adequately deal with that; after all, we are running Social Security surpluses right now.

If we were just looking at the Social Security system and enacting a balanced budget for that system we would say, well, we have gone beyond where we have to go, let us get rid of the surplus.

And, yet, we know that even with the surpluses we are currently running in the Social Security system, we are going to run out of money in about 30 years and there are going to be a lot of retirees then who are either going to have to take a cut in benefits or a lot of working people who are going to have very large payroll tax increases.

So, a Balanced Budget Amendment for Social Security would not do the trick. And, since Social Security and other entitlements are really what this is all about, having a Balanced Budget Amendment is not the way to deal with the problem.

Senator MOYNIHAN. Mr. Chairman, the vote is two to two, a tie vote.

The CHAIRMAN. Do I break the tie?

Senator MOYNIHAN. You have the last word.

The CHAIRMAN. Well, I want to pursue their questions a bit further. As you mentioned, within reason—and I think they all sort of agreed—the level of taxation is not as critically relevant as what you are spending money on. And if it is mainly transfer payments, you are likely to be less competitive than infrastructure and education. I would assume with a level of taxation of 80–90 percent, you would have a different answer, but within the bounds we are talking about.

But it is the transfer payments that are the ever—increasing portion of our budget. Medicare, Medicaid, Social Security, and other retirement are all transfer payments. Then you add interest to it, which is a transfer payment. They are 59 percent of our budget now, and they will be 68 percent in 10 years.

Now, you know the debate about consumption versus savings and investment, and the argument is our Tax Code tilts toward consumption and not enough towards savings and investments. First, do you even agree with that premise? And I will start at this end this time with Mr. Niskanen.

Mr. NISKANEN. Yes. Yes.

Mr. HUBBARD. Yes, absolutely.

Dr. FOSTER. Yes, sir.

Mr. AUERBACH. Yes.

Senator MOYNIHAN. Unanimity.

The CHAIRMAN. Two, if we were to tilt towards savings and investment, properly done—and we will get to what is properly done in a minute—would that be good for the future job production, quality of job, productivity, competitiveness of the country? And I will start at this end with Mr. Auerbach.

Mr. AUERBACH. Without doing anything to the structure of spending, if you were to keep the level of taxation the same and shift from income to consumption taxation, I think that would be a shift in the right direction, but I think it would leave major fiscal problems in terms of competitiveness.

The real problem we have is that we have a very large budget going toward transfers right now. In the long run, we are going to have to finance that. Even if you finance it with consumption taxes, you are still financing it with taxes. So, having very large deficits and shifting the tax from income to consumption may encourage private saving, but you have got a very big drag on national saving that remains.

The CHAIRMAN. I understand that.

Dr. Foster?

Dr. FOSTER. Yes. If properly done, shifting the tax off of saving and investment will definitely result in more saving and investment, which is a good thing.

Mr. HUBBARD. There are really two issues here. The movement toward a consumption tax is desirable for a number of reasons, one of which is the one you mentioned. However, the central problem in saving may not be the level of marginal tax rate on capital income so much as the structure of our social insurance programs and the inter-generational redistribution accompanying some of them.

The CHAIRMAN. What do you mean by that?

Mr. HUBBARD. In other words, we may be over-insuring individuals in some programs, and we are certainly redistributing resources across generations. The effects on savings from those programs may be significantly larger than the marginal effect of capital income taxation. This does not say that we should not worry a lot about capital income taxation and move to a consumption tax. However, we should not feel that we have "fixed" the problem unless we have tackled those entitlement programs.

The CHAIRMAN. Mr. Niskanen?

Mr. NISKANEN. Senator, one of the strongest patterns in economics is that the rate of economic growth across countries is very strongly correlated with the saving rate, and I think we need to change the tax policy, as well as change entitlement policies to increase that saving rate.

The CHAIRMAN. Now, when you use saving, can you add a conjunctive and say, and investment, or are those two different things, or do you assume they need to be the same?

Mr. NISKANEN. They are different to the extent of international capital flows. We have had a higher rate of domestic investment for 15 years than our domestic savings rate because we have been willing to borrow $150 billion a year from the Japanese, and previously the Germans. But there still is, both over time and across countries, a fairly high correlation between domestic savings rates and domestic investment rates.

Another word, here. It is important to distinguish the base of taxes from the incidence of taxes. When you tax consumption, that is the base of taxes, but the incidence still falls on factor earnings of some kind. The important thing to recognize is that, in the modern world, it is very difficult to tax the income from capital.

The increased globalization of the capital market means that the incidence of taxes is borne by the least mobile factor. So what we call taxation on capital, for the most part, is borne by American labor because capital has become much more mobile across borders.

We call it a corporate tax and we call it a capital gains tax and so forth. But, for the most part, it is a tax on American labor because that is the less mobile factor across borders.

The CHAIRMAN. And let me ask each of you this question, and we will start again with Professor Auerbach. Assuming we get a handle on entitlements—and I hope we do; I do not know if we are going to—and level off at least the rate of increase, give me some suggestions as to the best forms of increasing our savings and investment. What kind of laws could we pass to encourage it?

Mr. AUERBACH. You mean, affecting private behavior.

The CHAIRMAN. Yes.

Mr. AUERBACH. Holding deficit issues aside?

The CHAIRMAN. Yes.

Mr. AUERBACH. I would look, first, for ways of broadening the tax base that would be pro-saving by eliminating tax expenditures that encourage consumption and borrowing; further capping interest deductions, for example.

The CHAIRMAN. You mean, on what?

Mr. AUERBACH. On owner-occupied housing.

The CHAIRMAN. All right.

Mr. AUERBACH. That is primarily what is left.

The CHAIRMAN. Right.

Mr. AUERBACH. I would look for judicious use of consumption taxes, even if you keep income taxes at the same level or to reduce certain income taxes. If you do not want to switch entirely to a consumption tax, we can at least consider replacing part of the more complicated aspects of the income tax base with a value added tax, for example. Those are two suggestions.

The CHAIRMAN. Dr. Foster?

Dr. FOSTER. Yes. It depends a bit on the time frame in which you want to bring this about because there are certain things we can do fairly quickly because we know their parameters. We could have very large forms of IRAs, for example. We know how to legislate those and we know how to define them.

The CHAIRMAN. Should we?

Dr. FOSTER. Frankly, I think, yes, clearly, because we can do it fast. This is a long-term problem but that does not mean we should not do the things we know how to do soon. IRAs, I think, would fall under that category. I think capital gains reduction probably would fit under that category as well.

In terms of more longer-term change, a broad tax reform effort that, in general, removed the taxation from savings and investment is exactly what would fit the bill to increase private saving. The exact form that would take has many options. I do not really have a preference at this point between them.

The CHAIRMAN. Mr. Hubbard?

Mr. HUBBARD. Let me offer a conventional answer and an unconventional answer. The conventional answer is the one that you have more or less heard twice, which is to move from income taxation to consumption taxes. A short-run caveat I would offer in that conventional answer is that you try to avoid a short-term solution that makes it harder for you to get where you want to in the long run. Think about where you want to be in the long term, first.

The unconventional answer is, education. Most American families are woefully unaware of saving needs. Retirement is something——

The CHAIRMAN. In other words, you do not mean money spent on education, you mean educating families as to savings.

Mr. HUBBARD. Yes, educating about savings. Most American families are grossly unprepared for retirement decisions or what we might think of as precautionary decisions, saving for a rainy day, in large part because retirement is something most of us do once, maybe twice, but not experiencing the kind of learning we do in many of our economic decisions. Anything we can bring to bear through Social Security statements, or through an education campaign about saving, I think, might have some very hard to quantify, but very positive, effects.

The CHAIRMAN. Where we saw that in spades was during World War II in the war bond drive.

Mr. HUBBARD. Absolutely, Senator.

The CHAIRMAN. We encouraged that. Pat and I can probably remember going to school and having put in your dimes and quarters for savings bonds, and the teacher took it to the post office or someplace, and we did it every week, and it encouraged tremendous savings in this country.

Mr. Niskanen?

Mr. NISKANEN. The Republicans have put three very interesting tax proposals on the table—the Nunn-Domenici plan, the Armey plan, the Archer plan—all of which would have significant positive effects on savings and investment. Unfortunately, the House Republican contract is not consistent with any of those important reform plans.

The CHAIRMAN. You mean the $500 tax credit per child, especially?

Mr. NISKANEN. Plus the other features of it, for the most part, as well. And I want to reinforce the position of Dr. Hubbard that, do not do things in the short-run that are inconsistent with where you think you ought to be going in the long-run.

The short-run decisions you approve this year should be beginning steps toward the reforms that you think are appropriate in the long run, so even if you are not prepared to address another substantial tax reform until, say, 1997, keep that form in mind when you review and approve measures this year.

The CHAIRMAN. Senator Moseley-Braun.

Senator MOSELEY-BRAUN. Thank you, Mr. Chairman. I will be very brief. I just want to say thank you very much for convening this hearing. It has been really delightful to listen to these experts talk about this subject, which should be interesting to everybody.

I could not help but think while sitting here, that I cook as a hobby. That is what I do. I mean, I enjoy cooking. One of the things that any cook will tell you is that if you start off with the wrong ingredients in the base, you have just ruined whatever it is you are going to try to do. So I was delighted to hear Mr. Hubbard touch on education. You did it specifically with regard to educating citizens and taxpayers with regard to savings, and that that is important. But I think underlying a lot of this, as we talk about our international competitiveness, as we talk about encouraging savings and investment as a part of this economy, that if we do not begin to face up on the fact that our population, our polity generally, the dumbing down of America, Senator Moynihan, that has been written about, our polity, generally, is beginning to enjoy a lesser degree of basic education. I do not care how much we change budget scoring rules and how much we change the Tax Code. Our country is going to be left behind in this next century vis-a-vis the other developing and industrialized countries of the world.

That is what is so frightening about a lot of this, is that more and more we have got this conversation going on among a few people, but the impacts of it, other than radio talk shows which will just make anybody crazy—I should not have said that, that was impolitic—but overall, the realities that you are talking about now are not being shared with the American people.

It just seems to me to be so critical that we have a reality check, that we make certain people understand what the basic ingredients are, so that we can begin to engage in dialogue or a conversation about those basic ingredients so we can reach consensus that will be productive, constructive, and consistent with what we are supposed to do in our jobs here.

So I just want to thank you, Mr. Chairman, and thank you, members of the panel. Again, I was delighted to hear education at least crop up in the conversation because it seems to me that we really almost have to start there.

The CHAIRMAN. Senator Moynihan.

Senator MOYNIHAN. Well, this is the first substantive hearing of the new Congress and the new era. We have had a roll reversal here, which is not for the first time. I think, given our new condition, I might just conclude my comments by citing the immortal observation of Dr. Johnson, who once said, "How few of all the ills that human hearts endure, that part which laws or kings can cause or cure."

The CHAIRMAN. That is a good comment to close on.

Gentlemen, thank you very much.

[Whereupon, at 11:19 a.m., the hearing was adjourned.]

APPENDIX

ADDITIONAL MATERIAL SUBMITTED

PREPARED STATEMENT OF ALAN J. AUERBACH

Mr. Chairman and Members of the Committee:

I am pleased to appear before you to discuss my views on the current process of revenue estimation. In particular, I will consider both the feasibility and the advisability of adopting a scheme of "dynamic" revenue estimation, which would account for the net revenue changes resulting from the macroeconomic consequences of policy changes.

After a brief review of how revenue estimates are currently produced and used, my testimony will assess the accuracy of current revenue estimates. I will consider how the revenue estimation process might be changed to improve their accuracy and the role that revenue estimates should play in the policy process. I reach the following conclusions:

1. Government revenue estimates have been very inaccurate during the past decade. Errors in predicting aggregate revenue and its components have been large, and forecasts generally have been too optimistic—actual revenue typically has fallen short of predictions.

2. Part of this error appears attributable to behavioral responses to taxation. Errors, particularly for corporate and excise taxes, appear to be systematically related to prior policy changes. However, some of the excessive optimism embodied in forecasts may also result from the pressures of the policy process.

3. Current budget rules need to be adjusted to reflect these forecasting difficulties. The present mechanism ignores the likelihood of forecast errors and provides no mechanism for anticipating or reacting to them.

4. Dynamic revenue scoring poses problems more complex than those already plaguing the estimation process. Moreover, there are logical reasons for separating such revenue changes from those currently being accounted for by the revenue estimation process.

5. Dynamic revenue scoring offers no guarantee of a "free lunch" in the evaluation of tax cuts. Indeed, under current economic conditions, general tax cuts that encourage consumption and reduce national saving will reduce economic growth and future tax revenues. Including these revenue effects will raise: not lower, the estimated revenue cost of tax cuts.

6. Just as short-run revenue estimates are accorded too large a role in the policy process, long-run estimates receive too little attention. As a result, policies are designed to shift revenues in order to mask their long-run cost, and the true magnitude of this nation's fiscal problems are ignored. Current long-run projections indicate that U.S. fiscal policy is terribly out of balance. Large tax cuts, even if fully financed by true reductions in government spending, are not an appropriate response to this problem.

THE CONSTRUCTION OF REVENUE ESTIMATES

There are two types of revenue estimates produced by government agencies: forecasts of the level of aggregate revenue and its components, and estimates of the impact of specific policies on revenues. The estimates for individual provisions are used in revising the estimates of overall revenue levels, and in determining whether particular pieces of legislation are in accord with budget rules.

Each year, the Congressional Budget Office (CBO) and the Office of Management and Budget (OMB) produce estimates of aggregate federal revenues and their components, such as corporate income taxes, individual income taxes, and excise taxes. Typically, these estimates cover not only the upcoming fiscal year, but also several future fiscal years. The estimates reflect baseline policy assumptions and forecasts of macroeconomic conditions, and are constructed using estimates of the effects of specific revenue provisions provided by the Joint Committee on Taxation (JCT) and the Treasury's Office of Tax Analysis (OTA), respectively.

Over time, the CBO and OMB projections are updated to reflect changes in policy and in macroeconomic forecasts. While the macroeconomic effects of revenue measures may ultimately be reflected in changed macroeconomic forecasts, these changes are not attributed to the policies when the revenue estimates are reported. For example, the JCT estimate of the revenue effects of a reduction in the gasoline tax will take macroeconomic conditions as given. When CBO revises its revenue forecast, it will attribute to the gasoline tax the JCT revenue estimate but not any additional change in revenues that might be indirectly caused by the tax policy's impact on macroeconomic conditions. Any indirect revenue effects will simply be attributed to changes in macroeconomic conditions without being traced back to the policies that might have caused the changes in macroeconomic conditions.

Thus, revenue estimates of policy changes are not "dynamic" in the sense that they do not include the macroeconomic feedback effects of tax policies, although the effects may ultimately be recognized in revising macroeconomic forecasts. On the other hand, revenue estimates are not purely static in nature, as they often incorporate projections of behavioral responses in affected markets or transactions. For example, the revenue estimate of a change in the capital gains tax rate will incorporate predicted changes in capital gains realizations, but not changes in output or investment that might also result from the tax change. In other words, the existing methodology directly accounts for micro! but not "macro" behavioral responses to taxation. Critics argue that legislative actions are distorted because current revenue estimating procedures take inadequate account of taxpayer behavior at the micro level and should be revised to incorporate changes at the macro level as well.

ACCURACY OF RECENT REVENUE ESTIMATION

It is difficult, in general, to evaluate the accuracy of individual revenue estimates produced by the JCT or OTA because typically many tax changes occur simultaneously and we cannot determine the extent to which forecasts of the effects of particular provisions were in error. We can, however, consider the accuracy of the overall forecasts of OMB and CBO. My recent review of these forecasts indicates that they have been overly optimistic and not particularly accurate in recent years.

Table 1 presents statistics on the accuracy of OMB's annual budget forecasts. It is based on information published in the federal budget regarding the most recently ended fiscal year, which breaks down forecast errors for each revenue source into three components, according to whether the error can be attributed to policy changes relative to baseline ("policy"), changes in macroeconomic conditions ("macroeconomic"), or neither of these reasons ("technical").

Table 1—Average OMB Forecast Errors, Fiscal Years 1982–93

[As a percentage of revenues]

Revenue Source	Source of Error			
	Policy	Macroeconomic	Technical	Total
Individual Income	−0.1	−1.9	0.4	−1.6
Corporate Income	4.5	−16.7	−6.7	−18.9
Excise	3.2	−7.0	−3.4	−7.2
Total Revenue	0.5	−3.1	−0.6	−3.2

The table shows that, on average, total revenues were overpredicted by 3.2 percent. Most of this average forecast error is attributable to overly optimistic macroeconomic forecasts. Excise taxes and, especially, corporate taxes, were forecast with greater error than individual income taxes. In each of these two cases, policy changes were judged on average to have raised revenue in excess of baseline forecasts, but revisions attributed to macroeconomic and technical errors were, on average, quite negative. These errors reflect overly optimistic macroeconomic forecasts and significant overpredictions of revenues beyond those resulting from changing macroeconomic conditions. Leaving aside changes in revenue attributed to policy, corporate revenue predictions were 25.6 percent too high, on average, and excise tax predictions were 10.4 percent too high.

In considering the magnitude of these errors, it is important to keep in mind that these are not long-range predictions, but forecasts made less than a year before the fiscal years in question. One would expect forecasts made several years into the future to involve even greater error. Indeed, in a recent paper I found that aggregate macroeconomic and forecast errors of CBO 5-year revenue forecasts averaged $123.8 billion dollars annually over the period 1983–93.[1]

Why have revenue forecasts been so inaccurate and overly optimistic? At least part of the story does seem to relate to behavioral effects. While this is a subject in need of further investigation, initial findings indicate that the technical OMB prediction errors for corporate and excise taxes have been systematically related to prior policy changes. That is, when corporate or excise tax revenues increased as the result of tax policy changes—as they often did during the period 1982–93—the estimated revenue increases turned out to be too optimistic.[2] But this is not the whole story: even after correcting for apparent behavioral effects, significant year-to-year forecast errors remain and are difficult to explain. In short, we are very limited in our ability to make accurate predictions, even short-term ones.

IMPLICATIONS FOR BUDGET SCORING

These findings have several implications for the design of budget rules and the use of revenue estimates. First, and most obvious, is that the limitations of the estimation process must be recognized. Consider the analogy to meteorology, a science that economists often choose for comparison because of its forecasting difficulties. We are willing to accept the uncertainty that meteorologists present us with when they indicate that there is a 60 percent chance of rain tomorrow, and that it is difficult to know what the weather will be next week. We benefit not only by knowing that it might rain but also by knowing that this is only a possibility. The same should be true of revenue estimates. If there is a large margin of error around a particular estimate, then the margin should be made explicit so that policy deliberations can account for the fact that things might turn out much better or much worse. If mechanical budget scoring Nles can operate only if precise estimates are provided, then these rules simply should not be used: precise estimation is impossible.

Second, policy decisions should take account of the persistent overoptimism of past forecasts. Current budget rules only permit changes in tax policy that, according to estimates, will not increase the size of the deficit. Experience strongly suggests that more stringent rules may be needed to balance the potential overoptimism of revenue estimates.

Third, a more thorough examination of past forecasting performance would be helpful in determining the extent to which future performance can be improved by the incorporation of additional behavioral effects.

SHOULD DYNAMIC REVENUE SCORING BE USED?

In adopting what has been called the "dynamic" revenue scoring method, Congress would add to existing revenue estimates any additional revenue (or subtract any loss of revenue) calculated to result from the macroeconomic changes attributable to the tax policy. In principle, the concept of dynamic revenue estimation is attractive: why not account for all revenue effects rather than just some? In practice, I foresee several difficulties confronting a move to dynamic revenue estimation.

The most serious problem in the application of dynamic revenue estimation is the uncertainty surrounding estimates. Moving from particular markets to the economy as a whole introduces an entirely new set of problems for the revenue forecaster. Even in cases in which there is reasonably good evidence about the elasticities of supply and demand in particular markets, there is relatively little information about the extent to which contraction or expansion in particular markets affects aggregate macroeconomic activity. For example, we may form reasonable estimates of the extent to which a tax on tobacco will reduce tobacco production and consumption, but it is far more difficult to know how much, if at all, this reduction of economic activity in one market will change output as a whole. The answer depends on a number of questions, such as the flexibility of labor markets, the overall state of the macroeconomy, and the response of the Federal Reserve to changes in economic conditions.

In many instances, honest estimates of the macroeconomic feedback effects of many policy changes would amount to little more than educated guesses. In the current environment, in which each estimate has immediate ramifications for policy,

---

[1] Alan J. Auerbach, "The U.S. Fiscal Problem: Where We Are, How We Got Here, and Where We're Going," in *NBER Macroeconomics Annual 1994,* eds. S. Fischer and J. Rotemberg (Cambridge: MIT Press).

[2] Alan J. Auerbach, "Tax Projections and the Budget: Lessons from the 1980s," paper presented at the American Economic Association annual meetings, Washington, January 6, 1995.

this would amount to allowing the nation's tax policies to be dictated by the guesses of overworked government economists. On the other hand, having little or no anchor in economic evidence, these estimates would be more susceptible to political pressure than current estimates are. What government revenue estimator will wish to hold back the tide of legislative zeal with an educated guess?

Political pressure aside, there are logical reasons for keeping separate account of the macroeconomic effects of policy changes. After all, if at ax policy stimulates growth in income, society gains much more than the extra tax revenue on that income. Presumably, this is why growth-oriented polices are attractive. But if one includes the impact of economic growth among the benefits of a tax policy, then it is double-counting to subtract part of this growth from the policy's costs.

Finally, given the current state of discussion, it is important to recognize that dynamic revenue estimation would not necessarily reduce the estimated revenue cost of tax cuts. For example, an income tax reduction unaccompanied by significant reductions in marginal income tax rates on labor supply and saving would affect aggregate economic activity primarily by increasing household consumption. Given the economy's current position near full capacity, this increase in consumption would have little impact on output; it would simply crowd out other private purchases, namely exports and investment, thereby reducing the rate of wealth accumulation and income growth and the tax revenues of future years. Stimulating consumption is not equivalent to stimulating growth. Most tax-cut policies would increase consumption spending without stimulating growth.

FOCUSING ON THE LONG TERM

My final conclusion is that we need to give more weight to the long-term effects of fiscal policies. Given the inaccuracy of short-term forecasts and the greater inaccuracy of medium-term forecasts, the idea of looking even further into the future may seem paradoxical. Yet current budget rules exaggerate the gap between our knowledge about the short term ad about the long term. These rules assume we have perfect knowledge about near-term events and no knowledge at all about the future. In fact, our near-term knowledge is imperfect and our longer-term information, though even less accurate, is of some value.

In ignoring the long-run consequences of enacted policies, budget rules bias policy toward provisions that, by chance or design, have more favorable revenue consequences within the budget window than beyond it. Even if we cannot predict a policy's exact revenue effects, often we can discern a temporal revenue pattern that portends ill for the future. Shifting of revenue losses beyond the budget window has become a widely practiced art, and the young and future generations that are its victims can offer little opposition to those practicing it. Sanctifying with budget rules legislation chat punishes future generations simply encourages the abuse.

Given current projections of entitlement spending growth, the United States faces an inevitable fiscal crisis of enormous proportions that can be addressed today only by significant, permanent reductions in the federal budget deficit. Reductions in the deficit will not be facilitated by budget rules based on short horizons, optimistic projections and the unrealistic hope of induced growth.

PREPARED STATEMENT OF J.D. FOSTER, PH.D.

Mr. Chairman, Members of the Committee, my name is J.D. Foster, and I am the Executive Director and Chief Economist of the Tax Foundation. It is a pleasure to be before the Committee again. I thank the Committee for the opportunity to appear today to discuss the prospects for improving congressional revenue estimates through dynamic scoring.

The Tax Foundation is a non-profit, non-partisan research and public education organization that has been monitoring fiscal policy at all levels of government since 1937. We have approximately 600 members, consisting of large and small corporate and non-corporate businesses, charitable foundations, and individuals. Our business membership covers practically every region of the country and every industry category.

When it was established in the 1930s, the Tax Foundation's founding fathers set out certain principles of taxation which the Tax Foundation would promote and which would guide our analysis of tax proposals. According to these principles, a good tax system should:

- Be as simple as possible—complexity makes accurate tax compliance needlessly expensive and diminishes the public's willingness to comply with the law;
- Not be retroactive—taxpayers must have confidence in the law as it exists entering into a transaction;

- Raise revenue, not micromanage the economy with subsidies and penalties;
- Not be continually rewritten—frequent change lessens citizen understanding of the tax code and complicates long-term economic planning; and,
- Be implemented recognizing the competitive nature of the world economy.

I commend the Committee for meeting to hear economists argue over the esoterica of revenue estimates. And I appreciate the patience required to sift through debate about the current practice, what I call "nearly static" scoring, versus "dynamic" scoring, particularly when there should really be no debate. Accepting the limits of human knowledge, Members should be able to take the accuracy of these estimates for granted. But instead, Members have had to take for granted that the estimates have often been systematically in error. Further, Members have been consistently told by the Treasury, by the Congressional Budget Office (CBO), and others that these errors are unfortunate, negligible, and in any case unavoidable, and that the basic methodology for estimating revenues should not be changed.

Let me just say—I disagree, and I am not alone. Among others, the current President of the National Bureau of Economic Research and former Chairman of the President's Council of Economic Advisers (CEA), Dr. Martin Feldstein, has written recently that he believes we should move towards dynamic scoring, as does Dr. Michael Boskin, another former Chairman of the CEA.

Before I discuss the nature and advantages of dynamic scoring, a few disclaimers are in order. First, given the rules under which they operate, the techniques and models employed by the Treasury and the Joint Tax Committee (JTC) are extraordinarily complex instruments developed over years of refinement and based on some of the best data known to economists.

Second, I believe the estimators are first-rate professionals who strive to find the right answers given the tools available.

Third, just to be clear, the estimators do not generally produce "static" estimates. A static estimate would be one in which the taxpayer is assumed not to change behavior in response to a change in tax. In contrast, the JTC frequently accounts for the most immediate response of taxpayers to a change in tax. For example, a gasoline tax increase is assumed to reduce the amount of gasoline consumed, thereby producing less revenue than if gasoline consumption were assumed to be unaffected.

Fourth, dynamic revenue estimating is not nor will it ever be a magic wand capable of solving our fiscal problems. There may be unique instances in which a tax reduction can produce enough of a beneficial effect on the economy that a nearly static tax cut can be shown through dynamic analysis to be a revenue raiser. But there may also be no such cases, and, in most cases, "tax cuts" will reduce federal receipts and "tax increases" will raise tax receipts.

And, finally, whereas the current nearly static methods occasionally produce revenue estimates that are demonstrably in error, dynamic scoring will only yield more accurate estimates if the additional "feedback" effects are incorporated into the estimates correctly.

The Congress might be thought of as the Captain of a great ship called the U.S.S. Federal Tax Policy, setting the destinations as you sail the seven seas of alternative tax policies. The revenue estimators may be thought of as the navigators, providing course and speed to reach the destination you set. The raw data used by the estimators are the charts and soundings. And the models they use are their compass, clock, and sextant. Today, the sextant can't get the angles right and the clock tends to run a little fast. So no matter how hard they may try, using these tools your navigators cannot get you to your destination except by chance.

Some will tell you nothing can be done—no repairs are needed or possible. That position would be unacceptable under any circumstance, but the fact is we do know how to make significant repairs and we will learn more once we start. And you will see your chances of bringing your ship into port dramatically improved.

The goal is to produce the most accurate estimates possible so that Members can once again take the numbers for granted and focus on tax policy. The point is that dynamic scoring, done with circumspection, can produce significantly more accurate estimates than are currently available.

THE PROBLEM EXEMPLIFIED

As the JTC and Treasury correctly claim, the current estimates are not truly static. Great care is taken to ensure that the most immediate reaction of taxpayers in a market subject to a tax change is incorporated into the revenue estimates. Unfortunately, the consequences of those reactions and all other reactions are ignored. This can best be explained by way of example. Two additional examples are provided in the appendix dealing with a capital gains exclusion and raising the Social Security earnings limit.

A LITTLE BOAT HISTORY

In 1990 the Congress enacted the luxury boat tax, which was subsequently repealed. I use this tax as an example, not because it was good or bad tax policy, nor because the revenue estimates associated with the tax were more or less accurate than any other, but because the enactment of this tax created a relatively well-defined experiment in revenue estimating.

The 1990 Omnibus Budget Reconciliation Act levied a 10 percent excise tax on the value of boats and yachts in excess of $100,000 when those boats were not used for a business purpose. A truly static estimate of the receipts from this tax would apply the 10 percent rate to the estimated value of all personal boats that would be sold in the U.S. over $100,000 in value if the tax had not been enacted. In other words, if 2,000 boats that cost an average of $150,000 would have been sold, then a truly static estimate would project additional revenues of $10 million annually [($150,000 − $100,000)x2,000x10 percent].

The JTC assumed a reduction in the number and value of the boats sold and produced a correspondingly smaller revenue estimate. Continuing with the example, the JTC might have assumed sales would decline by 5 percent, to 1,900 boats sold, thereby reducing the revenue estimate to $9.5 million. The degree of demand response assumed by the JTC can certainly be questioned, and the industry certainly raised many questions, but the first point is that the JTC acknowledged the immediate market reaction to the tax and adjusted its estimates *of excise tax collections accordingly*.

Further, when it recognized that fewer boats would be sold, the JTC also allowed that some boat builders would go out of business, that workers employed in these firms would lose their jobs, that suppliers to these former boat builders would experience a decline in their business, and so forth. Unfortunately, in the world of nearly static revenue estimating, these effects have no consequences for income tax payments, payroll tax collections, excise tax receipts, or any other revenue source of the federal government.

The JTC assumed that all workers who once built boats immediately found employment at the same wages in other occupations; that capital previously employed in boat building was instantaneously employed in producing some other commodity; and that the former suppliers to the now-defunct boat builders immediately began to supply the new businesses that sprang up to replace the old boat builders.

In equilibrium, the JTC's implicit assumption that all these factors of production will be employed again at their previous wage and profit levels is arguably appropriate. In application, such an assumption may be reasonable, at least to a first approximation, over a three- to five- to ten-year horizon, depending on the state of the national and local economies. But to assume such a frictionless and immediate transition is unreasonable.

The consequences for federal receipts (and outlays) in the first years following the tax change were surely dramatic. Whatever receipts were estimated from the excise tax were initially offset, in part, in whole, and possibly many times over, by the loss of other receipts. When these businesses went under, they ceased paying income tax. When the employees lost their jobs, they ceased paying income tax and payroll tax. In fact, their unemployment checks alone may have cost the government more revenue than was projected from the excise tax.

Therefore, to argue about whether or not the tax raised as much revenue as projected misses the point. We must look at tax proposals comprehensively, looking at the big picture or else the estimates should not be used because they mislead. Even if the luxury boat tax collected the revenues projected, the other tax receipts that were lost, and the additional expenditures that were incurred (all of which were ignored in the official estimates) certainly lowered projections and conceivably cost the Treasury more than the tax itself brought in.

The question is not whether the CBO's baseline projections for GDP growth over the next five years should be raised or lowered a tenth of a point. For narrow tax changes, dynamic scoring would require recognizing a fuller range of consequences of tax policy—making reasonable assumptions about how markets as a whole will be affected by a change in policy. Dynamic scoring recognizes that jobs, wages, and profits are affected by tax policy and attempts to measure these effects in terms of federal receipts.

For broad tax changes, dynamic scoring is about whether the economy will employ more or less capital, whether individuals will save more or less, whether more or fewer people will choose to enter the labor pool and whether there will be jobs waiting for them. And, if the magnitude of these effects is sufficient, then they will appear in the CBO projections of aggregate GDP. Dynamic scoring should not be seen as a top-down procedure, working from CBO projections downward, but rather as a bottom-up method that recognizes how individuals and markets respond to changes in taxation.

THE ARGUMENTS AGAINST DYNAMIC SCORING

Defenders of the current methodology have raised a number of issues that deserve serious consideration, including the negligible macroeconomic effects of many tax proposals; our poor understanding of the magnitudes of many feedback effects; the potential for dynamic scoring to lead to increases in the budget deficit; the need to be consistent between revenue and spending methodologies; the need to maintain the credibility of the estimates; and the need to inoculate the estimating process from manipulation.

Macroeconomics versus Dynamic Scoring

A common argument against dynamic scoring is that a great many tax proposals have no measurable macroeconomic effect, so that there is no point to performing a dynamic estimate. This argument is exactly half right—many proposals have no *measurable* macroeconomic effect, but that has nothing to do with whether these same proposals should be estimated accounting for the broadest possible range of microeconomic feedback effects.

The methodology of nearly static scoring varies by tax proposal because some proposals, such as changes in individual tax rates, allow the JTC to use its base models, such as those for individual or corporate taxpayers, while other proposals, such as the luxury boat tax, are too narrow for these models and require the development of more specific models.

In an ideal world employing dynamic scoring, meaning one in which our understanding of markets and the data available are far greater than they are today, the JTC would have one great model of the economy which it could use or adapt as needed to estimate whatever tax proposals might arise. In the meantime, however, we will have to settle for dynamic analysis using some general models and some specific models, just as we do today. For example, a change in the individual income tax rate would have a wide range of effects on labor participation rates, saving rates, the cost of capital, and so forth. The consequences of these effects for GDP can be estimated to Produce a measure of the proposal's macroeconomic effects. At the outset, conservative estimates of these feedback effects would be most appropriate, and, over time, as our knowledge and data improve, these estimates will become more refined and more accurate.

For narrower proposals, more targeted models will be required as they are now. Again, using the luxury boat tax as the example, a dynamic scoring of this tax would require the development of an industry-specific model to account for the businesses that fail, the workers who go on unemployment, and all the revenues that are lost as a consequence.

The Limits of Understanding

A common joke is that if you lined up 100 economists from end-to-end you would never reach a conclusion. And there is some truth to that. There is a great deal we do not know about how individuals and markets react to various changes in prices and other circumstances. And there are very few tax proposals around which a consensus among economists exists regarding a *point* estimate of taxpayer response.

But just because we do not know everything does not mean we know nothing. To do nothing because we do not know everything is to make the "best" the enemy of the "good." Economists have studied how individuals react to changes in their economic environment for hundreds of years. And while disagreements abound about precise estimates, there is broad agreement on ranges of response for many cases. For example, no one knows exactly how taxpayers will change their net saving behavior in response to a new type of Individual Retirement Account. But we know there will be a response id research exists to suggest a range within which the precise figure likely falls. The JTC's current methodology assumes a zero response, which certainly falls outside the range suggested by prior research. Thus, the revenue estimates will without question be more accurate if they assume even the minimum degree of taxpayer response suggested by this research.

And, while we may not know exactly how an increase in private saving will affect the economy and federal receipts, we do know there will be effects on interest rates, investment levels, the trade deficit, employment, personal income, and tax receipts. It would obviously be better to project these consequences and their revenue effects conservatively than to ignore them altogether. Any improvement in accuracy remains an improvement. Further, our understanding of the economy, markets, and individual behavior grows every year. As additional research produces more complete results and more robust estimates, this work can be used to refine our modeling of the feedback effects.

Not long ago, if you had said you wanted to fly, you'd be told it can't be done. And if the Wright brothers had accepted that, then flight would have been discovered years later. But it would have been discovered, because eventually somebody would have taken what was known, done a little research, and the headlines would have read—it can be done.

When the test pilots in California were going faster and faster following the Second World War, some said you couldn't go faster than the speed of sound, that it was an impenetrable wall. But the engineers, as is their habit, did not listen to those who said it couldn't be done, and they designed a plane and found a pilot and the sound barrier was broken.

It is true that economists do not have the exact answer to every question of how taxpayers will react, either singly or as a group, to every tax change under consideration. But we do have approximate answers, ranges, to a wide variety of tax changes. Though we do not know all the answers, we should not ignore the answers we do have. If mankind had taken the same attitude towards flight that some have taken towards dynamic scoring, the Members of this Committee might be taking the train back to visit your constituents.

Dynamic Scoring and the Budget Deficit

Perhaps at no time in our nation's history has the budget deficit achieved more importance than it has today. It is, therefore, understandable that concerns would be raised about the potential for dynamic scoring to mask the true consequences for the budget deficit of a change in policy. If, for example, a proposal to reduce a tax is estimated using dynamic scoring, and if the actual loss in revenue proves to be much larger than the estimate, then the budget deficit would increase relative to what had been expected when the legislation was enacted.

This argument cuts both ways. For example, suppose the Congress intended to raise a tax to pay for a certain amount of additional spending, and that the Congress relied on a nearly static estimate of the revenues raised by the tax increase to ensure that the budget deficit did not increase. It is very likely that the additional revenues actually received as a result of the change in tax policy would be much less than what was estimated, and the budget deficit would increase as a result of this new program. Similarly, suppose the tax was increased in order to achieve a certain amount of deficit reduction. By using nearly static scoring, the Congress will have used an estimate that overstates the amount of revenue to be received and, therefore, less deficit reduction will occur than was expected.

Thus, the choice between nearly static and dynamic scoring is itself almost neutral when it comes to the budget deficit. Nearly static scoring is certain to produce a higher budget deficit than anticipated when a tax is increased, while dynamic scoring may produce a higher deficit when a tax is reduced. The difference is that the method used virtually guarantees that nearly static estimates will overstate revenue increases, whereas any time dynamic estimates understate revenues foregone it would only be because the estimators' models were not sufficiently refined.

Consistency Between Taxes and Spending

Both taxes and spending can affect economic performance. Specific spending programs from government R&D to farm price supports and the child immunology program all have advocates to argue that there are offsetting budgetary benefits to their programs. And many of them may be right.

The point is and must always be to get the numbers right so that the public and policy makers can make informed decisions. If a spending program can be shown to have clear secondary budget effects within the relevant budget window, whether because they cause other program costs to fall or because they increase national output, then these benefits should be recognized and the cost of the program adjusted accordingly. To be sure, these secondary budget benefits may be harder to isolate and estimate than is the case with many tax proposals, but where such information is available it should not be ignored. Under no circumstance, however, should dynamic scoring of specific spending programs be considered a prerequisite for dynamic scoring of tax proposals.

Credibility and the Manipulation of the Figures

Despite the use of nearly static estimating procedures, the estimators have maintained a remarkably high degree of credibility which can, I believe, be attributed to their professionalism. One source of their credibility is the perception of their unwillingness to modify their estimates in the face of political pressure.

However, the estimators' credibility has eroded somewhat in recent years because their methods fail to account for a wider range of feedback effects. In some instances, this refusal has produced estimates that were plainly absurd, such as the exchange the Chairman had with David Brockway, then Staff Director of the JTC, in 1983 over the enormous revenues that were estimated to result from a 100 percent individual income tax rate.

This erosion continues and is likely to accelerate in the future as more and more people become aware—through the press, through professional discussions, and through hearings such as this—of the obvious theoretical and practical shortcomings of nearly static scoring.

The JTC's credibility would be significantly enhanced if it published its models and its assumptions, and if it set out on a program of developing the capability to generate dynamic revenue estimates. The publication of its methodologies and assumptions would clearly open JTC estimates to criticism and review. But this process would itself tend to improve the accuracy of the estimates and would alleviate all suspicions that the estimates are not based on sound reasoning or may be subject to manipulation.

The crux of the credibility concern is, of course, that the use of more dynamic scoring methods could open the revenue-estimating procedures to political pressure and manipulation. It is reasonable to argue, however, that even if the estimators are entirely immune from such undue influence today, the methods they employ are by their nature not as neutral as we would all like. Because they fail to account for a fuller range of dynamic responses, the current methodologies ignore the deleterious consequences of tax increases and the beneficial affects of tax reductions. It would be naive, at best, to suggest that such a system is politically neutral.

Further, there is nothing inherently political about using a more dynamic analysis. Indeed, since the goal is to get the most accurate numbers possible, and since dynamic scoring, properly done, holds out the strong likelihood of improving the accuracy of the estimates, it is fair to argue that dynamic scoring is the only system that can completely de-politicize the numbers.

In practice, however, due care would have to be taken to assure that the methods adhere to the best understanding available of the economy and how markets would respond to particular tax changes. The best way to achieve this is, again, to publicize the methods and assumptions of the estimators. In the meantime, and possibly in addition, the JTC should consider establishing a body of outside experts specifically to work with the JTC as a sounding board and quality check.

Recommendations

In conclusion, I offer three simple recommendations. First, the Congress should recognize that a wide range of feedback effects can and should be taken into account in estimating the change in revenues from a change in tax policy.

Second, everyone involved should recognize that neither the JTC nor, for that matter, the Treasury, will be able to switch over to dynamic scoring immediately. This is a technology that will have to be mastered over time and applied where possible and where appropriate.

Finally, having decided to go forward with this new technology, the Congress should establish a working group including representatives from the JTC, the CBO, the Senate Finance and the House Ways and Means Committees, and a small number of outside experts to develop a business plan for moving to dynamic estimates. Among other things, this working group will need to determine:

- The principles to be used in performing a dynamic analysis;
- A set of rules for determining when dynamic analysis should be used;
- A timetable for expanding the range of proposals qualifying for dynamic scoring;
- The additional staffing requirements needed to meet the timetable;
- Possible new procedures for interactions between the JTC and CBO;
- Procedures for publicizing JTC methods and assumptions; and
- The structure and responsibilities of an outside council of experts who will advise the JTC in developing its dynamic models.

Without such a working group it will be very difficult to assure that this new (to the Congress) technology is made available to the tax policy process. If the estimators had begun this in the early 1980s, the Congress would today be deliberating tax proposals with the benefit of estimates that would be far more accurate and in which you could have a justified confidence. Many are predicting that, in the next few years, we will be continuing the evolution of the federal tax system with a quantum jump known as a tax reform. I remember, and I am sure the Chairman does even more clearly, how central to the process were the revenue estimates. No one knows what form the tax code will take, but it is certain we are more likely to achieve the policy goals set if the revenue estimates are closer to the mark. And this requires that we begin the transition to fully dynamic scoring today.

APPENDIX

This appendix provides two additional examples of how dynamic revenue estimating differs from the current, nearly static methodology. These examples are chosen to illustrate the nature of the estimating process and not to imply an advocacy of the change under consideration. The examples considered include a capital gains exclusion, raising the Social Security earnings limit, and a general tariff reduction.

The Capital Gains Exclusion

The Congress has considered various forms of capital gains exclusion since the enactment of the 1986 Tax Reform Act. Four revenue effects follow.from such a proposal: an exclusion effect, a realizations effect, a price effect, and a growth effect. Of these four, the current estimating procedures account for the exclusion and realization effects with great precision and detail, and ignore the price and growth effects altogether.

A taxable capital gain arises when an asset is sold that has appreciated since its time of purchase, that is, when the capital gain is realized. Of the four effects, the exclusion effect is the easiest to understand and to measure. Quite simply, given a level of net capital gains realizations, a 50 percent exclusion would reduce by half the amount of realizations subject to tax.

In a given year, taxpayers own a certain body of assets which have appreciated in price. From this pool of appreciated assets they will sell a certain dollar amount on which will arise a certain dollar amount of taxable capital gains. For each taxpayer, the decision to sell an asset may be the product of many factors, one of which is the tax on capital gain that may be owed. Clearly, the higher the rate of tax the less disposed the taxpayer will be to sell a tax-bearing asset. The effect of a capital gain exclusion is to reduce the effective rate of tax, and thereby reduce the disincentive to sell the asset. Consequently, all else held equal, a capital gains exclusion will increase the rate of capital gains realizations.

Few issues in tax policy have been so thoroughly researched empirically as the change in capital gains realizations following a change in the effective tax rate. And, despite the differences in their estimates, the Treasury Department and the JTC actually use very similar estimates of taxpayer response so that the difference in their estimates is statistically meaningless, even though the difference in dollar terms may be quite large.

One effect neither Treasury nor the JTC account for is the price effect of capital gains relief. An asset's price is determined by the discounted value of all after-tax proceeds from that asset. Clearly, for any asset inclined to increase in price, a lower capital gains tax will produce a higher asset price. Therefore, any reduction in the effective capital gains tax rate will surely produce a general increase in asset prices, thereby increasing the current pool of unrealized capital gains, thereby further increasing the dollar volume of capital gains realized in a given year and increasing the aggregate amount of capital gains tax paid.

Finally, capital gains relief is proposed because it is expected to reduce the tax disincentives to save and invest, ultimately producing stronger economic growth. While the degree to which a given capital gains proposal will have this beneficial effect is debatable, the existence of the effect itself is not. Nevertheless, the official estimates make no effort to include even the slightest additional growth effect in their calculations. Moreover, this effect would manifest itself not only in terms of higher subsequent capital gains tax receipts, but also as higher receipts from virtually every tax and fee imposed by the federal government.

Even if the combination of the exclusion and realization effects reduces federal receipts as the official estimates predict, when we add in the combination of the price and growth effects, then most exclusion proposals as have been suggested in recent years would almost certainly produce higher federal receipts in both the short run and the long run.

The Social Security Earnings Limit

The Social Security earnings limit applies to taxpayers under 70 years of age and reduces their Social Security benefits by one dollar for every three dollars they earn over a specific threshold. The earnings limit, therefore, is the economic equivalent of a 33 percent income tax surcharge on those affected. Any raising of the earnings limit threshold or the benefit-loss ratio reduces the effective tax disincentive facing the elderly who wish to continue to earn labor income. Such a change would also, in the first instance, increase the federal outlays for Social Security benefits, thereby increasing the budget deficit.

Raising the earnings limit would have other, revenue increasing effects, as well, which are not included in the official estimates. For example, if an elderly individual chooses to work more following the increase in the earnings limit, he or she will be subject to payroll tax on the earnings. Thus, while the amount of benefits paid increases, so, too, does total payroll tax receipts.

Also, the General Fund of the Treasury would receive an increase in individual income tax receipts as the elderly would likely have larger amounts of income subject to income tax. In fact, the elderly are likely to pay more of a wide variety of federal levies if they choose to work longer following the raising of the earnings limit. In combination, each of these effects may not cause the increase of the Social Security earnings limit to reduce the budget deficit on net, but they certainly would reduce the amount of the deficit increase relative to the official estimates.

Prepared Statement of Glenn Hubbard

Chairman Packwood, Ranking Member Moynihan, and other distinguished members of this Committee, I am pleased to join you today to share my observations and suggestions on procedures for estimating the revenue consequences of legislative proposals. I have worked with the Treasury Department, Office of Management and Budget, and Committees of Congress on this issue, and I offer observations and suggestions on the basis of careful consideration.

In my remarks, I consider five issues for information and discussion: (1) effects of legislative proposals on federal revenues, (2) current revenue estimating methodology, (3) the pros and cons of incorporating dynamic "macrofeedback" effects in estimating procedures, (4) information required to develop estimates with macrofeedback effects, and (5) studying and developing a more comprehensive revenue estimating procedure.

EFFECTS OF LEGISLATIVE PROPOSALS ON FEDERAL REVENUES

Much of the discussion surrounding revenue estimates centers on the distinction between "static" and "dynamic" estimates. In fact, there are three categories of revenue estimates of proposals. The first relates to the effect of the tax change on revenue for a given baseline. The second and third relate to how the baseline itself may respond to the tax change.

Static Estimates. Given current taxpayer behavior, how would a proposed tax change affect revenues? For example, if there were no change in the amount of capital gains realized, how much revenue would be foregone as a result of a cut in the rate of tax on capital gains.

Microdynamic Estimates. How would the proposed tax change affect revenues by changing taxpayers' behavior? For example, if the capital gains tax rate were reduced, what would be the revenue gain when individuals responded to the lower tax rates by realizing more capital gains?

Dynamic Macrofeedback Estimates. How would the proposed tax change affect revenues by changing the rate of growth of the overall economy? For example, how much incremental revenue would be obtained if additional income-generating investments were made as a result of a lower tax rate?

CURRENT REVENUE ESTIMATING METHODOLOGY

Revenue estimates for individual proposals embody both static and microdynamic elements just defined; that is, revenue estimators attempt to predict many types of taxpayer responses to the tax change, in addition to estimating the revenue effect of the proposal given the initial tax base. This prediction involves making assumptions about "behavioral responses' to policy changes. For example, the well-publicized difference between revenue estimates prepared by the Joint Committee on Taxation and the Treasury Department's Office of Tax Analysis for the Bush administration's capital gains tax proposals reflects greater microdynamic responses in the administration's estimates.

Though not commonly understood, some broad revenue estimates incorporate macrofeedback effects. The administration's budget receipts baseline incorporates the collective effects of the administration's budget proposals on the overall level of economic activity—that is, the macrofeedback effect of all of the proposals taken together. In that sense, the budget reflects the effects of the administration's proposals on economic growth and federal receipts and outlays.

SUGGESTED CHANGE IN ESTIMATING PROCEDURES

As I noted earlier, the current presentation of the budget does not quantify separately the macroeconomic feedback effect of each proposal embodied in the budget, nor do the revenue estimates for individual proposals made separately during the year include their macroeconomic feedbacks. This reflects current and longstanding practice. It also highlights the principal issue under discussion, namely that tax policy proposals—and particularly major growth-oriented policies—may independently affect overall economic activity and that congressional and administration revenue estimates should take this into account.

The basic arguments in favor of including dynamic macroeconomic feedbacks for individual proposals are the following:

- Tax policies can affect saving, investment, and economic growth, which in turn affect federal tax revenues. Policies that stimulate growth should be "given credit" for their effects on the overall level of economic activity, while policies that hinder growth should have their negative effects recognized.
- Although dynamic revenue estimates would be imprecise, even imperfect estimates might help enactment of growth-oriented proposals—that is, those that generate positive macroeconomic feedbacks.
- Although dynamic revenue estimates are more difficult and controversial than those prepared under current procedures, they might be done only for major proposals.

The basic arguments that have been made against this approach include the following:

- Economists' models are imprecise: As a practical matter, macrofeedback effects attributable to any single proposal cannot be estimated with much certainty. Because such estimates are imprecise, the macrofeedback effects could be used to support proposals that would inflate the federal budget deficit.
- The same arguments would logically apply to macrofeedback effects for expenditure or social policy proposals. For example, proponents might claim that a substantial expansion of various spending programs would have no net cost to the government—because they create jobs and therefore generate revenue, or reduce other outlays and therefore save the government money.
- Including macrofeedback effects in revenue estimates would carry political risks (for example, charges of manipulating budget estimates) and/or economic risks (if the financial markets concluded the effort was being used as an attempt to abandon budget discipline).
- Information and personnel requirements would be substantial. From the administration's perspective, the Council of Economic Advisers, Office of Management and Budget, and Treasury Department would have to produce the new economic forecast that reflects the macrofeedback effects of each legislative proposal examined. The Treasury Department's Office of Tax Analysis would have to estimate revenue effects of proposals using the new economic forecast that would include feedback effects. In the Congress, a similar interactive process would have to be managed by the Congressional Budget Office and the Joint Committee on Taxation.

Major policy proposals do, of course, have an impact on economic activity and federal tax receipts. For example, during the Bush administration, the Council of Economic Advisers and the Treasury Department testified regarding the beneficial impact of a reduction in the tax rate on capital gains on investment and economic growth. Other examples of major policy proposals include integrating the corporate and individual income tax systems and switching from an income tax to a consumption tax.

I recommend that you initiate a study of how and under what circumstances "dynamic" revenue estimates might be prepared. (I return to this point below.) This study should emphasize the application of any revised procedures to the analysis of major proposals. Many policy proposals generate sufficiently small economic effects that measuring macrofeedback effects would be unimportant. The Treasury Department and the Joint Committee on Taxation could devise de minimis rules for dealing with such proposals.

STUDYING AND DEVELOPING MORE COMPREHENSIVE ESTIMATING PROCEDURES

Having raised issues related to "dynamic scoring" per se, I would like to place "revenue estimation" in a broader context of tax policy analysis. In the course of your deliberations over individual policy proposals or collections of policy proposals, you consider how such proposals affect the level and distribution of economic well-being—of present and future members of our society. As these deliberations occur, revenue estimates help the Congress (or the administration) determine the magnitude and scope of the proposal under consideration. In addition, under the present rules governing the budget process, revenue estimates are used to inform the Congress (or the administration) about the consequences for budget deficits in the short term of the proposal's enactment.

I have four concerns with this current use of "revenue estimates" in the tax policy process.

A revenue estimate is only an estimate. Each revenue estimate prepared by the staff of the Joint Committee on Taxation or the Office of Tax Analysis reflects the best prediction of the effect of a particular proposal on revenues over a period of time, currently five fiscal years. Staff economists consult available data and academic studies in the course of preparing revenue estimates, often under extreme time pressure. The considerable uncertainty in revenue estimates suggests the usefulness of presenting a range of revenue effects of a policy proposal in addition to "the" revenue estimate.

Assumptions matter. Let's suppose for the moment that we enter nirvana for revenue estimators (and academic economists), in which estimates can be made without statistical error. Suppose a tax increase raises a given amount of revenue. How will those funds be used? To reduce other taxes? Increase spending? Will the tax change be temporary or permanent? Despite revenue estimators' efforts, there is no single correct set of assumptions, and conventions sometimes adopted in the revenue-estimating process can lead to misleading results.

Revenue estimates should inform policymakers of the long-run consequences of proposals under consideration. By this, I mean that policymakers should be informed of the effect of the proposal on the present value of revenue to the government (or, at least, on revenue accruing over a suitably long period of time). Such information can guide the design of policies to emphasize long-run consequences over short-run timing effects. The present budget enforcement rules make this information particularly valuable for tax-writing committees and the administration.

Improvements to revenue and distributional analysis should be coordinated. Just as information presented in revenue estimates should present analysis of the long-run consequences of proposals, distributional analysis should move beyond one-year or five-year horizons. Recent research by economists has focused on measuring lifetime burdens of tax policies and examining intergenerational redistributions accompanying tax policies. While none of these approaches is without its flaws, lengthening the horizon for distributional analysis provides essential information for decisionmakers.

With these concerns in mind, I encourage you to initiate a review of current revenue-estimating procedures. A key goal of such a review should be the development of a revenue impact statement, which would present conventional revenue estimates (that is, over a "budget window" period), a discussion of consequences of the proposal beyond the short term, an analysis of macrofeedback effects (if significant), and a discussion of broad efficiency and distributional effects of the proposal. (In principle, such impact statements could be prepared for tax-equivalent mandates and regulations as well.)

Under the present budget rules, such a revenue impact statement would provide valuable information for this Committee. Any discussion of whether to apply macrofeedback effects for revenue scoring" purposes as well should be part of a broader deliberation over budget procedures.

As part of my suggested study of macrofeedback effects, I suggest that you ask revenue-estimating staffs and outside economists to prepare an estimate of "dynamic" effects of certain major policy proposals, including a significant reduction in the capital gains tax rate, the enactment of a permanent investment tax credit, and a switch from income to consumption taxation. The range of such estimates among forecasters along with the uncertainty surrounding each one will give you more precise information about the usefulness of incorporating macrofeedback effects in official budget scoring procedures, as opposed to simply including them in a revenue impact statement. As you deliberate, I encourage you to seek common ground between procedures employed by the Joint Committee on Taxation and the Treasury Department's Office of Tax Analysis.

CONCLUSION

Revenue estimates provide important information to policymakers about the consequences of tax proposals. As I have argued, however, the limited information offered to satisfy the current budget scoring rules fails to give policymakers all of the relevant information about revenue, distributional, and efficiency effects of tax proposals to facilitate sound decisionmaking.

Dynamic revenue estimating, while perhaps the most visible concern at the present time, is only one of several significant issues requiring attention if you decide to reform revenue-estimating conventions. I urge you to study such reforms (including analyzing the desirability and feasibility of dynamic revenue estimating), especially with an eye toward designing informative revenue impact statements. I would urge you not to incorporate macrofeedback effects in official revenue estimates, even for major policy proposals, prior to reviewing revenue estimating procedures more broadly.

Thank you for your attention and consideration.

METHODOLOGY AND ISSUES IN THE REVENUE ESTIMATING PROCESS

Scheduled for a Hearing
Before the

SENATE COMMITTEE ON FINANCE
ON JANUARY 24, 1995

Prepared by the Staff
of the
JOINT COMMITTEE ON TAXATION

JCX-2-95
January 23 , 1995

CONTENTS

PAGE

INTRODUCTION

The Senate Committee on Finance has scheduled a public hearing on the revenue estimating process used to determine the effects of proposed tax legislation on fiscal year budget receipts (typically referred to as the revenue effects).

This pamphlet*, prepared by the staff of the Joint Committee on Taxation, discusses the revenue estimating process. Part I of the pamphlet is an overview and summary. Part II describes the revenue estimating methodology currently used by the Joint Committee staff, including key factors impacting the preparation of revenue estimates and behavioral effects taken into account in preparing revenue estimates. Part III discusses estimating methodology relating to certain tax legislative proposals. Part IV discusses issues relating to estimating the macroeconomic effects of proposed legislation. Part V provides a summary of testimony presented at the joint hearing of the House and Senate Budget Committees on estimating methodology held on January 10, 1995.

---

* This pamphlet may be cited as follows: Joint Committee on Taxation, Methodology and Issues in the Revenue Estimating Process, (JCX-2-95), January 23, 1995.

I. BACKGROUND AND SUMMARY

A. Background

The Joint Committee on Taxation staff ("Joint Committee staff") plays an integral role in virtually every stage of the tax legislative process. One aspect of this role involves estimating the effects of proposed tax legislation on fiscal year budget receipts, typically referred to as the revenue effects. Although this portion of the Joint Committee staff's work utilizes significant amounts of staff resources and is highly visible, it by no means constitutes the sole work of the staff.[1]

In performing its estimating function, the Joint Committee is guided by three principles. First, the objective of the estimating process is consistently to produce accurate estimates that can be reasonably relied upon by Members of Congress in making legislative decisions. Second, the Joint Committee staff is dedicated to continuously improving its estimating methodology to enhance the accuracy of its work product. Third, the Joint Committee staff is highly sensitive to the need for the estimating process to be viewed as fair and impartial.

This pamphlet focuses on an issue that has attracted significant attention to the work of the Joint Committee staff in recent years -- the methodology employed by the staff when estimating the effects on Federal budget receipts of tax legislation considered by Congress.

B. Summary

1. Revenue estimating methodology

<u>How revenue estimates are calculated</u>

Revenue estimates measure the anticipated changes in Federal receipts that result from proposed legislative changes to Federal tax laws.

Each proposal is estimated using essentially the same methodology. First, one must determine the revenue projected to be collected under present law. Second, one must estimate the revenue yield that would result from the proposed law. The difference between the two is the revenue estimate.

---

[1] For a summary of the history of the Joint Committee on Taxation, the work of the Joint Committee staff, and the role of the Joint Committee staff in the tax legislative process, see <u>Written Testimony of the Staff of the Joint Committee on Taxation Regarding the Revenue Estimating Process for the Joint Hearing of the House and Senate Budget Committees of the 104th Congress on January 10, 1995</u> (JCX-1-95), January 9, 1995, Appendix I.

For most revenue estimates, the Joint Committee staff relies on large computerized models of the Federal tax system and the economy. Basically, these models contain two components: (1) a calculator, which computes taxes paid under present law and under the proposal, and (2) tax return or other data. The primary data source for most models is tax returns filed with the Internal Revenue Service (IRS).

Behavioral effects

One of the most significant elements of revenue estimates is the assumed effect of taxpayer behavior. Although Joint Committee staff microsimulation models account for certain taxpayer behavior, additional adjustments are often necessary. In general, a revenue estimate prepared for any proposal that changes the treatment of an item of expense or income, or the rate of tax on certain types of income or consumption, will incorporate behavioral effects. Thus, Joint Committee staff estimates are dynamic to the extent they take into account direct behavioral responses that can be expected from proposed changes in the law.

Examples illustrating the manner in which Joint Committee staff estimating methodology accounts for behavioral changes include the following: excise tax increases are assumed to result in lower sales of the taxed items; a reduction in the capital gains tax is assumed to increase realizations; and changes in individual income tax rates are assumed to affect portfolio management decisions.

Macroeconomic effects

Traditional estimating conventions utilized by the Joint Committee staff assume that tax law changes will have no overall effect on economic aggregates such as gross domestic product (GDP). However, it is assumed that employment and investment may shift among sectors or industries, depending on the nature of the tax proposal.

2. Estimating methodology relating to certain proposals

Examples of some recent revenue estimates prepared by the Joint Committee staff illustrate issues that arise in revenue estimating, particularly the extent to which taxpayer behavior is taken into account.

Capital gains

Of the revenue estimates prepared by the Joint Committee staff in recent years, none has attracted more attention than the estimates of proposals to reduce the rate of tax on capital gains. The Joint Committee staff estimates of capital gains tax cut proposals assume significant increases in realizations from the rate change, both on a short- and long-term basis. Consistent with current estimating methodology, the Joint Committee staff does not take into account the possible macroeconomic effects of capital gains tax cut proposals. Such effects, if any, would be expected to come from increases in productivity resulting from changes in the capital stock. If such growth in productivity occurred, it would occur slowly at first, with most of the effects outside the five-year budget window.

Luxury tax

The luxury tax enacted in 1990 imposed a 10-percent excise tax on certain cars, boats, aircraft, furs, and jewelry. The Joint Committee staff revenue estimate assumed a significant change in consumption patterns stemming from the implementation of the excise tax, e.g., it assumed a significant decline in purchases of the tax items.

Proposals to increase the top individual income tax rate

As part of the Omnibus Reconciliation Act of 1993, two new individual income tax brackets of 36 percent and 39.6 percent were added, new alternative minimum tax rates were imposed, and the limitation on itemized deductions and the personal exemption phaseout were made permanent. The types of taxpayer behavior taken into account in estimating these changes included: the shifting from investments which yield interest and dividend income taxed at the new higher rates into investments that provide capital appreciation, which are taxed at unchanged lower rates; shifts from taxable to tax-exempt assets; use of different business form of organization; conversion of wage income into tax-deferred or tax-exempt employee benefits; and increased taxpayer noncompliance. While macroeconomic effects were not included in the estimates, it is not clear that they would have had a significant impact on the magnitude of the tax changes. In the case of changes in the top individual income tax rate, one would expect that the most probable macroeconomic effect would be a change in the labor supply of affected individuals.

3. Issues relating to estimating the macroeconomic effects of proposed legislation

As discussed above, the Joint Committee staff's current methodology does not predict the positive or negative effects, if any, a tax proposal might have on the overall economy. It has been suggested that, in making revenue estimates of a tax proposal, the Joint Committee staff should take into account the projected macroeconomic effects that would result from that particular tax proposal.

The Joint Committee staff has not included macroeconomic effects in its estimates for the following reasons:

- inclusion of macroeconomic effects in estimates of revenue proposals but not spending proposals could create an inconsistency in overall budget analysis;

- most revenue proposals are likely to have little or no macroeconomic consequences; and

- because of the complexity and lack of consensus as to the measurement of macroeconomic effects, attempting to take macroeconomic consequences into account could undermine the credibility of the estimating process and render estimates less reliable.

4. Summary of testimony before the joint hearing of the House and Senate Budget Committees

The House and Senate Budget Committees held a joint hearing on January 10, 1995, to examine the revenue estimating process. Kenneth J. Kies, Chief of Staff of the Joint Committee on Taxation, described the current revenue estimating methodology employed by the Joint Committee staff and discussed potential changes in the methodology. Robert D. Reischauer, Director of the Congressional Budget Office (CBO), presented the views of CBO. Witnesses at the joint hearing also included Henry J. Aaron (Director of the Economic Studies Program at the Brookings Institution); Michael J. Boskin (Professor of Economics and Hoover Institution Senior Fellow, Stanford University); Martin Feldstein (President of the National Bureau of Economic Research and Professor of Economics at Harvard); Alan Greenspan (Chairman, Board of Governors of the Federal Reserve System); Rudolph G. Penner (Managing Director of Barents Group LLC, KPMG Peat Marwick, and former Director of the Congressional Budget Office); Norman B. Ture (President, Institute for Research on the Economics of Taxation); and Paul A. Volcker (Former Chairman, Board of Governors of the Federal Reserve System). Excerpts of this testimony are contained in Section V.

88-270(92)

II. REVENUE ESTIMATING METHODOLOGY

A. Overview of The Joint Committee Staff's Current Revenue Estimating Methodology

1. The basic calculation of all revenue estimates

Revenue estimates measure the anticipated changes in Federal receipts that result from proposed legislative changes to the Internal Revenue Code or related statutes. The following discussion outlines the major elements involved in the revenue estimating methodology currently employed by the Joint Committee staff.

Requests for revenue estimates range from those affecting broad groups of taxpayers (e.g., proposals to exclude all interest and dividends from gross income or to adopt a value-added tax) to those affecting a narrow class of taxpayers (e.g., a proposal applicable only to the banking industry). Each proposal is estimated using essentially the same methodology. First, one must determine the revenue projected to be collected under present law. Second, one must estimate the revenue yield that will result from the tax law after it is modified. The difference between these two amounts is the revenue estimate.

2. The revenue baseline and macroeconomic forecasts

The reference point for a revenue estimate prepared by the Joint Committee staff is the Congressional Budget Office ("CBO") five-year projection of Federal receipts, referred to as the revenue baseline.[2] The revenue baseline serves as the benchmark for measuring the effects of proposed tax law changes. The baseline assumes that present law remains unchanged during the five-year budget period. Thus, the revenue baseline is an estimate of the Federal revenues that will be collected over the next five years in the absence of statutory changes.

The revenue baseline is based upon CBO forecasts of macroeconomic variables such as the annual rate of growth of nominal gross domestic product ("GDP"), inflation rates, interest rates, and employment levels. For modeling purposes, a number of elements of the CBO forecast are disaggregated to match specific tax-related variables. For example, the aggregate forecast of wages and salaries paid is statistically matched to various types of taxpayers by income class.

In contrast, the reference point for revenue estimates prepared by the Treasury Office of Tax Analysis ("OTA") is an alternative set of economic forecasts generated by the Administration. Differences in resulting revenue estimates prepared by the Joint Committee staff and by the OTA

---

[2] The revenue baseline is a component of the budget baseline prepared by CBO, which includes expenditures as well as receipts.

staff often can be traced to differences between the economic forecasts of CBO and the Administration.

As mandated by the Congressional Budget Act, revenue estimates published by the Joint Committee staff generally provide a fiscal year budget impact for the period ending five years following the current fiscal year (total of six fiscal years).[3]

B. Econometric and Statistical Simulation Tax Models

1. Models based on Statistics of Income data

For most revenue estimates of proposals to change the corpoate or individual income tax, the Joint Committee staff relies on large computerized models of the Federal income tax system and the economy. These models have been developed by economists on the Treasury OTA staff, the Joint Committee staff, and others. These models contain two components: (1) a calculator, which computes taxes paid under present law and under the proposal for which a revenue estimate is prepared and (2) tax return or other data. The primary data source for most models is the tax returns filed by individuals, corporations, and fiduciaries with the Internal Revenue Service ("IRS") and provided to the Joint Committee by the IRS Statistics of Income Division ("SOI"). The models combine the most recently available taxpayer information with forecasts of the aggregate level of national income provided by CBO.

The largest microsimulation model employed by the Joint Committee staff is the individual income tax model, which contains a random sample of approximately 200,000 individual income tax returns. This data is also matched with data from the Current Population Survey to account for individuals who do not file income tax returns. Once this match is complete, the file sample contains approximately 250,000 records. This sample is then statistically weighted to represent the entire filing and nonfiling population.

To estimate the revenue effects of most proposed changes in the individual income tax, the Joint Committee staff first uses the individual income tax model to calculate the tax liability for each of the sample returns in the model on the basis of present law. The model then recalculates the tax for each of the returns incorporating the parameters contained in the proposed legislation. In so doing, the model accounts for the interaction of all variable components of a taxpayer's return. For example, a 10-percent increase in the personal exemption does not necessarily increase the revenue loss associated with the personal exemption by 10 percent. Some returns will become nontaxable as a result of the increase, while other returns will shift to a different marginal rate bracket. The model will take these changes into account. After statistically weighting the

---

[3] A Senate budget rule (the so-called "Byrd rule") provides that a point of order requiring a 60-vote majority can be raised with respect to any legislation that is not budget neutral (1) in the first year, (2) in years one through five, and (3) in years six through ten.

present-law and proposed-law tax payments to adjust the results to reflect outcomes for the more than 110 million U.S. individual income tax returns, the model calculates the difference in total revenues between present law and the proposal. This result is often only the first step in estimating the revenue effect of a proposal. For example, as discussed below, the Joint Committee staff often must make further adjustments to account for changes in taxpayer behavior, to reflect interaction among a package of proposals, or to reflect fiscal year budget reporting.[4]

In addition to the individual tax model, the Joint Committee staff and the OTA staff utilize a corporate tax model and a depreciation model that are based on SOI tax return data.

2. Other models

The Joint Committee staff has developed a variety of econometric models to estimate the revenue impact of changes in tax laws relating to business investment and depreciation, natural resources and energy, employee benefits, and other issues. The information needed to calculate the revenue effects of a proposal may not be available from tax return data or may be available only for a limited number of potentially affected taxpayers. In these instances, the Joint Committee staff must look beyond the SOI data files and construct a model that relies on alternative sources of data.

Frequently, data may be available from other government agencies, such as the Department of Commerce, the Department of Transportation, the Department of Labor, the Department of Health and Human Services, the Social Security Administration, and the Federal Reserve Board. For example, the Current Population Survey conducted by the Bureau of the Census of the Department of Commerce provides useful and otherwise unavailable data relating to pension plan participation by income class.

In the absence of Federal or State government data sources, Joint Committee staff must locate other reliable sources, such as that available from leading economists, CBO, the General Accounting Office ("GAO"), private consulting or research organizations, or affected taxpayers.

---

[4] To be useful tools in budget analyses, estimates must be presented in a form consistent with the Federal government's cash-flow accounting system. Under this system, amounts received by the Treasury are accounted for at the time of receipt and disbursements are accounted for during the period when paid out.

To be consistent with the cash-flow measure of budget receipts, revenue estimates are shown in a format that corresponds to fiscal-year receipts of the Treasury Department. Because taxes are most often calculated on a calendar-year basis, the translation of changes in calendar-year tax liabilities into changes in the fiscal-year receipt of taxes is necessary.

C. Key Factors Affecting the Preparation of Revenue Estimates

After a microsimulation model produces a preliminary estimate of the revenue effect of a proposal, the Joint Committee staff often must make further adjustments to address issues that cannot be answered by directly applying the simulation models. These adjustments may be necessary to account for changes in taxpayer behavior (in addition to taxpayer behavioral effects calculated directly from the model), the interaction of various proposals, and issues relating to taxpayer compliance.

1. Anticipated behavioral responses

One of the most significant elements of Joint Committee staff revenue estimates is the assumed effect of taxpayer behavior. Although the microsimulation models used by the Joint Committee staff account for certain taxpayer behavior, additional adjustments are often necessary. In general, a revenue estimate prepared for any proposal that increases or reduces the deductibility or excludability of an item of expense or income, or that changes the rate of tax on certain types of income or consumption, will incorporate an analysis of potential behavioral responses. Thus, revenue estimates prepared by the Joint Committee staff are not static; Joint Committee staff estimates are dynamic to the extent they take account of the direct behavioral responses that can be expected from proposed changes in the tax laws.

In many cases, empirical research can offer guidance as to how taxpayers will respond to a proposed change in tax law. If adequate historical data exists (e.g., if a similar proposal was once included in the tax law), taxpayer response may be estimated statistically. For example, sufficient data is available to permit revenue estimates for proposals to change the excise tax on cigarettes to account for the expected change in demand for cigarettes.

Occasionally, reliable data will not be available to predict how taxpayers will respond to a proposed change. In such cases, the Joint Committee staff makes an informed judgment, relying on economic theory and other relevant sources, to assess possible behavioral responses.

The following examples demonstrate the ways in which the Joint Committee staff accounts for possible taxpayer behavior in preparing revenue estimates:

- When Congress limited the ability of taxpayers to deduct passive losses, the Joint Committee staff estimating methodology assumed that investment patterns would change and corporations would claim a portion of the losses no longer freely available to individuals. Thus, the Joint Committee staff estimated that the limitation on passive losses of individuals included in the Tax Reform Act of 1986 would raise $36 billion from individuals for the period 1987 to 1991, but would lose $12.6 billion from corporations during the same period.

- When the Tax Reform Act of 1986 made it less attractive for property and casualty insurance companies to invest in tax-exempt bonds, the Joint Committee staff assumed that these companies would shift partially from investments in tax-exempt bonds to higher yielding taxable investments, and that other corporations and individuals would acquire the tax-exempt bond holdings that insurance companies previously held. This phenomenon of investment shifting is an example of what are collectively referred to as "portfolio effects."

- Changes in excise taxes are expected to have an effect on sales of the taxed items. For example, the estimate of revenues to be gained from imposing the so-called "luxury tax" on boats, cars, airplanes, furs and jewelry assumed reductions in purchases of these items.

- Changes in the taxation of capital gains are assumed to affect how rapidly capital assets are sold. A proposed decrease in capital gains taxation will speed up the sale of capital assets, which moves some revenue into the budget window. Some of the speed up is assumed to be permanent; that is, it is assumed that some capital assets that might otherwise have been held until the death of the owner, thereby avoiding capital gains taxation entirely, are sold within the budget window as a result of a capital gains tax decrease. These changes result in increases in revenue, which offset much of the decrease from the tax cut.

- Other changes in the taxation of capital to provide specific incentives to acquire certain types of assets, such as targeted investment tax credits and accelerated depreciation, are also generally expected to affect investment decisions. These incentives are expected to speed up and, for some proposals, increase investment in the types of capital benefiting from the incentives. Investment in assets not entitled to the incentives is assumed to decline.

- Changes in individual income tax rates are assumed to affect portfolio management decisions of individuals. For example, an increase in the top individual income tax rate is assumed to result in increased holdings of tax-exempt bonds and reduced holdings of taxable investment instruments. To the extent that increasing the rate of tax on ordinary income reduces the taxation of capital gains relative to such ordinary income, it is assumed that individuals will shift portfolios so that they receive less current income as dividends and more as capital gains. Both of these assumptions reduce the estimated revenue gain from an increase in the top individual income tax rate.

- Changes in the deductibility of various expenses, such as home mortgage interest payments, business meals, or contributions to tax-deferred savings plans, are assumed to affect the rate at which such expenses occur. A decrease in the deductibility of business meals, for example, is assumed to reduce the total amount spent on business meals.

- Finally, for changes in tax law that may be difficult to enforce or administer, some efforts by taxpayers to avoid taxation are assumed. One such example is the provision included in the Energy Policy Act of 1992 to include in income the value of employer-provided parking to the extent that it is greater than $155 per month. The Joint Committee staff estimate assumed that there would be a tendency for taxpayers to take steps to reduce or underestimate the value of employer-provided parking so as to avoid income inclusion under this provision.

2. Interaction

When one proposal would modify two or more provisions within the Internal Revenue Code, the result of the combination of changes often produces a greater or lesser revenue effect than the sum of the revenue effects of each proposal if enacted separately. If this interaction is ignored, the analysis is incomplete; if the interaction is assigned to any one element of a proposal, the revenue estimate for that proposal may be misleading.

The proper interpretation of the revenues attributed to specific proposals and the accompanying interaction are determined by the "stacking order" of the analysis. There are two principal methods of presenting these results in line-by-line revenue tables, and it is important to note that the numbers in each type of presentation may appropriately answer different questions but reflect the same estimated revenue effect.

The first of these methods provides a revenue estimate for each proposal in isolation against present law, assuming none of the other proposals is adopted. A separate line on the revenue table displays interactions among proposals. This procedure is usually the most efficient when only a few proposed changes are involved. Under this method, deleting a proposal from the package may have a greater or lesser revenue effect than the effect shown on the specific line for that proposal.

A second method requires that each proposal be estimated as if all other proposals have already been enacted, with a separate line again displaying interactions among proposals. The Joint Committee staff utilized this second method to analyze the Tax Reform Act of 1986. This method showed the revenue impact of adding or deleting specific proposals from the total tax reform package (rather than the revenue impact relative to present law of that single change without making any of the other changes contained in the package).

3. Compliance and enforcement

Implicit in all Joint Committee staff revenue estimates are assumptions concerning compliance and enforcement. The revenue yield of any provision is dependent on the extent of compliance by taxpayers from both voluntary behavior and enforcement (including penalties assessed by the IRS). In general, levels of enforcement are assumed to remain unchanged as a result of most legislative proposals. However, many estimates do take into account changes in taxpayer compliance. This represents another aspect of taking into account behavioral effects.

Certain changes in tax law are specifically designed to improve compliance and also have the potential to affect enforcement. An example is the extension of information reporting to previously uncovered income sources. Information reporting generates compliance revenue by changing taxpayer perceptions of the risks of noncompliance and by assisting them in identifying the income they have received. In addition, the information reporting document could be of use to the IRS in the generation of enforcement revenues, either in the matching or audit process.

Revenue estimates of so-called "compliance" provisions do not always recognize both compliance and enforcement effects. The realization of compliance revenues in the example above requires only that the proposed change of law be expected to change taxpayer behavior. Thus, compliance revenues are included in the estimate. Downstream enforcement revenues, however, are dependent upon specific actions by the IRS, which may or may not occur depending on resource allocation decisions. Using the assumption of a constant baseline level of enforcement, such revenues would be "counted" only in the event of specific resource allocations, and not merely because of a change in law. Thus, in the above example, only the compliance revenue attributable to taxpayer behavior would be counted unless there were adequate resource allocations to justify counting the enforcement revenues.

D. Behavioral Effects and Macroeconomic Aggregates

1. Overview

The extent to which behavioral effects are taken into account in calculating the revenue effects of proposed tax legislation seems to cause the greatest confusion concerning the current estimating process. As discussed above, the Joint Committee staff does take many behavioral responses into account in preparing revenue estimates.

Revenue estimates often mistakenly are referred to as "static" because traditional estimating conventions utilized by the OTA staff and the Joint Committee staff assume no overall effect on economic aggregates such as gross domestic product; i.e., the forecast of total employment, investment, and other economic aggregates are assumed to remain unaffected by tax proposals. However, economists preparing revenue estimates assume that the components of these variables may change among sectors or industries, depending on the nature of the legislative proposal. For example, when the deduction for business meals was reduced, the revenue estimating methodology assumed some job displacement in the restaurant industry. However, it was assumed that this displacement was generally absorbed in other industries.

Ordinarily the growth of the following economic variables, as supplied by CBO, is assumed to be unchanged by proposed tax law changes for revenue-estimating purposes:

--Gross Domestic Product
--Aggregate investment
--Interest rates
--Overall price index
--Total level of State and local taxes

Although these aggregate levels are fixed in the CBO baseline, the composition of the variables underlying these aggregates may be assumed to vary as a result of a legislative proposal. Examples of elements of economic forecasts that may be reallocated include the following:

--Shifts between corporate and noncorporate income
--The mix of employee compensation between cash and nontaxable fringe benefits
--Relative prices of taxed versus non-taxed items

2. Behavioral effects not generally included in revenue estimates

The Joint Committee staff generally does not attempt to estimate the possible effects of a tax change on the growth of GDP. Use of a fixed revenue baseline means that, in developing revenue estimates, the Joint Committee staff does not take into account macroeconomic or "feedback" effects.

Thus, for example, with respect to tax changes that are likely to affect the return to capital, such as capital gains relief, investment tax credits, and accelerated depreciation, the fixed GDP forecast assumption means that the Joint Committee staff does not attempt to estimate growth in income resulting from the increased productivity, if any, caused by increases in investment. It also means the Joint Committee estimate does not account for any net increase in entrepreneurial activity generated by the incentives.

Similarly, the Joint Committee staff does not attempt to forecast changes in labor supply resulting from changes in income tax or payroll tax rates. At some income levels, the reduced disposable income resulting from an increase in tax rates could lead to an increase in labor supply by individuals seeking to maintain consumption levels. At other income levels, increases in tax rates may reduce labor supply as the marginal value of extra hours worked decreases. Hence, consideration of labor supply effects could increase or decrease the revenues to be anticipated from a tax increase, depending on whom the tax increase is affecting.

Some tax changes may affect the demand for labor. For example, excise tax increases that reduce demand for a product may result in layoffs in the affected industry. To the extent that the affected industry comprises a significant portion of a regional economy, such as tobacco in North Carolina, Virginia and Kentucky or "luxury" boats in New England, the reduced demand for labor could result in a local economic downturn. The resulting increased unemployment could generate additional Federal expense in the form of increased payments of unemployment compensation, food stamps, and other transfer payments. Joint Committee staff estimates do not reflect these effects.

Similarly, some tax incentives, such as empowerment zones and targeted jobs tax credits, target specific segments of the population likely to be receiving transfer payments from the Federal government. The budgetary effects of the revenue loss from these proposals may be offset by a reduction in Federal transfer payments, as well as by increased income and payroll taxes on any additional earned income. The Joint Committee staff does not attempt to account for these outlay effects in estimating such proposals.

The Joint Committee would not, in any case, attempt to measure such increases or decreases in transfer payments because they affect outlays for which CBO provides estimates.

III. ESTIMATING METHODOLOGY RELATING TO CERTAIN PROPOSALS

A. Overview

In an effort to further understanding of the issues involved in revenue estimating, the estimating methodology and issues relating to the following proposals are discussed below:

(1) Proposals to reduce the rate of tax on capital gains;
(2) The 10-percent luxury excise tax on boats, airplanes, jewelry, and fur enacted in 1990 and repealed in 1993; and
(3) Proposals to increase the top rate of tax on individuals.

The Joint Committee staff has provided revenue estimates for these proposals in recent years. They were chosen for discussion purposes in part because they have received considerable attention. They also illustrate some of the more complex issues that arise in the revenue estimating process.

B. Discussion of Specific Revenue Estimates

1. Proposals to reduce the rate of tax on capital gains

Of the revenue estimates prepared by the Joint Committee staff in recent years, none has attracted more attention than the estimates of proposals to reduce the rate of tax on capital gains. During the 1990 Budget Summit, significant attention was devoted to the differences in estimates of capital gains proposals prepared by the Joint Committee staff and the Treasury OTA staff.

A general overview of the methodology the Joint Committee staff utilizes to estimate capital gains proposals is presented below. In particular, there is a discussion of the two most significant issues to be considered when estimating capital gains proposals: (1) the extent to which enactment of a reduction in the rate of tax on capital gains will induce taxpayers to realize capital gains (the "unlocking effect"); and (2) the fact that current estimating methodologies do not account for possible macroeconomic effects of a proposed capital gains tax rate reduction.

The first step in estimating the revenue effects of a proposal to reduce the rate of tax on capital gains is to calculate the decrease in tax liability that would result from lowering the tax rate for baseline gains (i.e., those capital gains that would be realized even in the absence of a change in rates), measured without taking taxpayer behavior into account. This amount is calculated directly from the individual income tax model described above. In doing this calculation, the Joint Committee staff relies upon the forecast of capital gains realizations incorporated in the CBO baseline.

The second step takes into account induced realizations expected from the proposed rate change. Induced realizations represent the additional gains taxpayers are expected to realize as a result of a proposed lower tax rate on capital gains. These "induced realizations" are calculated by combining two factors: (a) the Joint Committee staff estimate of taxpayers' behavioral response to the proposed rate reduction (i.e., the assumed elasticity); and (b) the gain realizations reflected in the CBO revenue baseline. For many capital gains proposals, in the first few years after a capital gains tax rate reduction takes effect, the Joint Committee staff estimates that induced realizations will be more than sufficient to offset the revenue loss resulting from the lower rates, so that net Federal tax revenues are increased. However, the Joint Committee staff's estimates assume that this initial surge in realizations is temporary. Thus, the Joint Committee staff estimates that, after an adjustment period, in most cases taxpayers will settle into a more permanent level of realizations that will be lower than the initial surge, but higher than would be expected in the absence of a rate reduction.[5]

The Joint Committee staff has long recognized that a change in the rate of tax on capital gains will affect the level of capital gains realizations by taxpayers.[6] Economists use the term "elasticity" to describe the relative change in taxpayers' decisions to realize capital gains that can be expected in response to changes in the capital gains tax rate. Mathematically, the realization elasticity is the percentage change in realizations divided by the percentage change in tax rates.[7]

The Joint Committee staff estimate of the elasticity of taxpayer response to a reduced capital gains tax rate was developed after careful review of the major empirical and theoretical studies by experts in government and the academic community. The elasticities ultimately used, however, are not those reported in any single study; nor are they derived by a mechanical

---

[5] The current methodology of the Joint Committee staff in preparing distributional analysis of tax proposals, including capital gains tax rate cut proposals, includes increased tax revenue from the proposed changes for each of the five years of the budget period. This would include the tax from induced realizations in the case of a capital gains rate reduction.

[6] For example, in the General Explanation of the Revenue Act of 1978 (P.L. 95-600), the revenue table included a separate line item reflecting the increased revenues from induced capital gains realizations.

[7] For example, if a 10-percent reduction in the capital gains tax rate were expected to result in a 10-percent increase in realizations, the realization elasticity would be -1 (10 percent/-10 percent). An elasticity of -1.0 would mean that if the capital gains tax rate were lowered, the percentage increase in realizations would exactly offset the revenue loss from the reduction in the rate, resulting in no net revenue effect. An elasticity of -1.1 would mean that, if the capital gains tax rate were lowered, the increase in realizations would produce more revenues than the revenue loss occurring as a result of the lower tax rate. Similarly, an elasticity of -0.9 would mean that the increase in realizations from a reduction in the capital gains tax rate would be less than the loss of revenues from the lower rate.

averaging of any group of studies. Rather, they reflect the staff's independent evaluation of the results of the various studies, analyzed in the context of the historical record.

An important component of the Joint Committee staff realization elasticity is the "portfolio effect," which accounts for the ability of taxpayers to convert ordinary income to capital gain.[8] There are at least four ways in which this conversion can occur:

- Investors may select one type of asset rather than another, based on the type of income it is expected to produce. For example, investors may redirect their investment portfolios to replace assets that produce interest and dividends with assets that generate capital gains. As a consequence, dividend and interest income may decline just as capital gains income is increasing.

- Corporations may decide to pay out a lesser portion of their available earnings as dividends in the belief that greater retained earnings will translate into higher stock prices, generating more capital gain and less ordinary income for their shareholders.

- Employees may choose to replace salary income with capital gain income, for example, by choosing to receive stock or certain stock options as compensation in lieu of cash wages.

- Taxpayers may attempt to structure transactions - without affecting their economic substance - so as to realize their profits in a form which the tax law categorizes as capital gain rather than ordinary income.

Consistent with current estimating methodology, the Joint Committee staff does not take into account the possible effects of a capital gains tax cut on GDP (i.e., the macroeconomic or so-called "feedback" effects) in preparing revenue estimates of capital gains tax cut proposals. Such feedback effects on GDP, if any, would be expected to come from increases in productivity resulting from changes in the capital stock. Any such productivity growth would occur slowly at first, with most of the effects outside the budget window. In theory, increased entrepreneurial activity utilizing otherwise unemployed labor could generate short-run increases in GDP.

---

[8] Former and present members of the Joint Committee staff published an analysis of this point. Eric W. Cook and John F. O'Hare, "Issues Relating to the Taxation of Capital Gains," National Tax Journal, vol. 60, September 1987.

2. Estimates of the luxury excise tax

The luxury excise tax enacted as part of the Omnibus Budget Reconciliation Act of 1990 imposed a 10-percent excise tax on the value of automobiles in excess of $30,000, the value of boats in excess of $100,000, the value of personal-use aircraft[9] in excess of $250,000, and the value of furs and jewelry in excess of $10,000. The tax was effective for sales occurring on or after January 1, 1991. As part of the Omnibus Budget Reconciliation Act of 1993, the tax on boats, personal-use aircraft, furs, and jewelry was repealed. The repeal was effective for purchases of boats, jewelry, furs, and personal-use aircraft occurring on or after January 1, 1993. The 10-percent tax on automobiles was indexed periodically for inflation such that, in 1994, the tax applied only to the value of automobiles in excess of $32,000.

The methodology used to estimate excise tax proposals generally involves several steps. Once the initial tax base is determined, the base is adjusted to account for changes in consumption patterns (elasticities of demand and supply) that result from the imposition of the tax. The base is also adjusted to account for any significant compliance problems in the administration of the proposed tax. The tax rate is then applied to the adjusted tax base to yield the expected gross revenues from the tax.

One of the most fundamental components of any revenue estimate is the construction of the tax base. Estimation of the luxury excise tax proposal required information on units of each item sold at a given price. Because no single data source contained all the information necessary for the estimates, several data sets were used to derive the revenue estimates of the tax.

At the time of the legislative consideration of the luxury tax in 1990, little information was available from academic literature or from the affected industries on the elasticity of demand for cars, boats, jewelry and furs, and personal-use aircraft with values in excess of the proposed excise tax thresholds. Based on the available information, the Joint Committee assumed that demand for these items was highly elastic. Thus, the Joint Committee staff revenue estimate assumed a significant change in consumption patterns stemming from the implementation of the tax, i.e., it assumed a significant decline in purchases of the taxed items. Furthermore, the Joint Committee staff estimate assumed that some purchases of luxury goods which were otherwise planned to occur after the implementation of the tax were accelerated to avoid the tax. The Joint Committee estimate also assumed an initial period of lower than usual tax collections based upon an anticipated low level of compliance with the tax.

A comparison of estimates shown in the table below demonstrates that the luxury excise tax in fact produced more revenue than was expected in its first two years. This was due to the unexpectedly large receipts from the tax on automobiles. In addition, the tax on boats and jewelry

---

[9] Aircraft for which 80 percent of use was for nonpersonal activities were excluded from the tax.

produced more than the anticipated revenues in the first two years of the tax. The tax on furs generated the expected revenues for the 1991-1992 tax period, while the tax on personal-use aircraft generated less revenue than was anticipated. The table below compares the original Joint Committee gross revenue estimates from 1990 for the luxury excise tax with the actual tax receipts collected by the IRS.

IRS LUXURY EXCISE TAX RECEIPTS COMPARED TO JCT ESTIMATES[10]
Fiscal Years
[Millions of Dollars]

Items	1991(a)	1992
Airplanes over $250,000:		
IRS Actual Receipts	0.1	0.4
JCT Estimate	1.0	4.0
Shortfall	-0.9	-3.6
Boats over $100,000:		
IRS Actual Receipts	7.3	12.4
JCT Estimate	4.0	9.0
Excess	3.3	3.4
Automobiles over $30,000:		
IRS Actual Receipts	151.5	296.5
JCT Estimate	27.0	69.0
Excess	124.5	227.5
Furs over $10,000:		
IRS Actual Receipts	0.3	0.7
JCT Estimate	(*)	1.0
Shortfall	0.0	-0.3
Jewelry over $10,000:		
IRS Actual Receipts	9.2	15.8
JCT Estimate	1.0	3.0
Excess	8.2	12.8
Total:		
IRS Actual Receipts	168.4	325.8
JCT Estimate	33.0	87.0
Total Excess	**135.4**	**238.8**

(a) Year contains only 9 months of receipts.
(*) Gain of less than $1 million.

[10] The Joint Committee staff estimates provided in this table are the original estimates used in the Omnibus Budget Reconciliation Act of 1990 presented on a gross basis. IRS tax collection data represents gross fiscal-year excise tax collections. The net revenue estimates usually produced by the Joint Committee staff must be shown on a gross basis to produce any meaningful comparison.

Since the enactment of the luxury excise tax, there has been much debate about its effect on the boating industry. Data from the National Marine Manufacturers Association shows that the boating industry was in a recession two years prior to the enactment of the luxury tax. Beginning in 1989, the boating industry began to experience a significant decline in sales for both luxury and nonluxury boats. Between 1988 and 1990, sales of luxury and nonluxury boats declined by about one-third.[11] This decline continued through 1993. It has been asserted that several factors contributed to the decline in sales, including the lack of consumer confidence due to the oncoming recession, the luxury tax, State sales taxes, and a large used boat market from which lower priced substitutes were available. In 1993, anticipated repeal of the luxury excise tax caused a delay in the planned purchases of boats until 1994. The imposition of a luxury excise tax on boats would be expected to result in a reduction of luxury boat sales. The Joint Committee estimate of the luxury excise tax on boats took account of such a reduction in sales on top of an already declining industry.

3. Proposals to increase the top individual income tax rate

As part of the Omnibus Reconciliation Act of 1993, two new individual income tax brackets of 36 percent and 39.6 percent were added. In addition, new alternative minimum tax rates were imposed and the limitation of itemized deductions and the personal exemption phaseout were made permanent.

The estimation of these changes began with the use of the individual income tax microsimulation model, described previously, to calculate the change in tax liability resulting from the proposed changes. The model provides the forecast distribution of income which is essential to the calculation and accounts for interactions between the provisions.

The model output was then adjusted after considering certain behavioral responses on the part of affected individuals. This adjustment was particularly critical in this case because the provisions affected high-income individuals who are generally assumed to have greater access to information and greater ability to rearrange their affairs to minimize the impact of the tax.

The types of taxpayer behavior taken into account include the shifting from investments which yield interest and dividend income, taxed at the new higher rates, into investments that provide capital appreciation, which is taxed at unchanged lower rates. Also considered were shifts from taxable to tax-exempt assets, conversion to C corporation business form, conversion of wage income into tax-deferred compensation or tax-exempt fringe benefits, and increased noncompliance and avoidance.

In making the determination of how much behavioral response to include, the Joint Committee staff reviewed available studies and consulted with the OTA staff. The final result was a reduction in the estimate of increased fiscal year receipts of $8.5 billion or a reduction of approximately 7 percent of the change in receipts projected by the microsimulation model, for the five-year period.

---

[11] GAO Report - Tax Policy and Administration: Luxury excise tax issues and estimated effects, February 1992; GAO/GGD-92-9.

Because all revenue estimates assume fixed levels of macroeconomic aggregates, the behavioral responses considered did not include actions which would affect the overall output of the economy such as a change in the supply of labor. While macroeconomic effects were not included in the estimate, it is not clear that they would have had a significant impact on the magnitude of the tax change. In the case of changes in the top individual income tax rate, one would expect that the most probable macroeconomic effect would be a change in the labor supply of affected individuals.

IV. ISSUES RELATING TO ESTIMATING THE MACROECONOMIC EFFECTS OF PROPOSED LEGISLATION

A. In General

As indicated above, under current revenue estimating methodology, a revenue estimate predicts how Federal receipts will increase or decrease relative to the baseline projections if a proposed change in the tax law is enacted. However, although a revenue estimate under current estimating methodology may incorporate anticipated behavioral responses to a proposed change in the tax law, the estimate does not take into account the potential effect the proposal may have on aggregate economic growth, interest rates, or other macroeconomic variables. Thus, revenue estimates prepared under the current methodology do not predict the positive or negative effects, if any, a proposal might have on the overall economy.

It has been suggested that in making revenue estimates of a tax proposal, the Joint Committee staff should take into account the projected macroeconomic effects that would result from that particular tax proposal.

B. Issues to be Considered Concerning the Possibility of Incorporating Macroeconomic Effects in Revenue Estimates

There are a number of important issues which need to be analyzed in considering whether to modify the current estimating methodology applicable to proposed tax policy changes to take into account possible macroeconomic effects.[12] The following are key issues that should be considered.

1. Consistency between revenue estimates and spending estimates

Inclusion of macroeconomic effects in estimates of revenue proposals but not spending or regulatory proposals could create an inconsistency in overall budget analysis. Many proposed changes in spending and regulatory policy could have a structural effect on the economy, changing the long-run potential for growth of GDP. It is possible, for example, that a proposed reduction in the taxation of income from capital investments might be balanced by a proposed reduction in certain Federal infrastructure expenditures. Many economists believe that a cut in spending on infrastructure will result in a reduced rate of growth in GDP. To the extent that a change in taxes is offset by a change in spending, a budget forecast that incorporates the long-run growth effects of the tax cut, but not those of a corresponding cut in spending, will produce a biased picture of the effects of the proposal on the Federal budget deficit.

---

[12] These issues are discussed in more detail in the Congressional Budget Office (CBO) Publication Budget Estimates: Current Practices and Alternative Approaches (January 1995), prepared by CBO as background for a joint hearing on budget estimation procedures held by the House and Senate Committees on the Budget on January 10, 1995.

In the short run, a tax cut could stimulate the economy by providing consumers with more disposable income, which would result in more demand for products, and thus more production. However, in near full-employment economies, such as the current one, this effect will be reduced by rising interest rates caused by the increase in the Federal deficit. To the extent that a tax cut is balanced by a spending cut, economists would expect to see a reduction in demand caused by the reduced purchases of goods and services by the Federal government. If the Joint Committee staff were to attempt to incorporate such cyclical demand analysis in revenue estimates, it would present a biased picture of the effects of budget legislation on the Federal deficit unless CBO also incorporates cyclical demand effects in its analysis of expenditure changes.

2. Small macroeconomic impacts of most proposals

Most revenue proposals are likely to have little or no macroeconomic consequences. The vast majority of revenue proposals analyzed by the Joint Committee staff may be expected to affect small sub-sectors of the economy. They will result in shifting of resources from one industry to another, but will not signficantly affect total national income. For example, a reduction in the allowable deduction for meals and entertainment would reduce restaurant sales. But the money that would have been spent in restaurants will either be spent elsewhere, or will add to the stock of savings, thus increasing taxable income in other segments of the economy. The net effect of the provision on macroeconomic aggregates would be negligible for revenue estimating purposes.

Some proposals, such as cuts in capital gains taxes and accelerated depreciation schedules, that increase the after-tax returns to capital, may be expected to affect the long-run growth rate of GDP. But it is likely that the effects of this capital build-up will develop gradually, with most of the budgetary consequences occuring outside the five-year budget window. Even a ten-year forecasting horizon may not be long enough for the full effects of increased productivity resulting from increased capital accumulation to be fully manifested. The only net growth effects that are likely to occur within the budget horizon are those resulting from increased entrepreneurship. Such activity has been a very small factor in previous market responses to changes in the taxation of income from capital.

3. Lack of consensus among economists about forecasting macroeconomic effects

There is little consensus among economists about the exact nature or magnitude of likely macroeconomic responses to many types of fiscal policy changes. Because of the complexity and lack of consensus as to the measurement of such macroeconomic effects, attempting to take macroeconomic consequences into account could undermine the credibility of the estimating process and render estimates less reliable.

The uncertainty of monetary policy further contributes to this problem. Demand-generated fluctuations in GDP will only materialize if the Federal Reserve Board does not attempt to counteract them with its own changes in policy. Therefore, successfully predicting these cyclical demand effects would also require accurate prediction of corresponding Federal Reserve monetary policy actions and their effects on the economy. To the extent that the Federal Reserve does work to counteract the effects of fiscal policy on aggregate demand, tax cuts will have very little demand-driven macroeconomic effect.

In addition, although magnitude and direction of the economy's response to actions by the Federal Reserve is generally more predictable than the economy's response to fiscal policy, the timing of the response to monetary policy is very difficult to predict. Timing is as important in revenue estimating as magnitude, given the pay-as-you-go requirements of the budget act. The uncertainty inherent in predicting the timing of monetary policy effects on the economy further compromises the reliability of revenue estimates that incorporate cyclical demand effects.

According to some economists, a decrease in taxes on income from capital will result in a significant increase in income due to increased productivity and, possibly, increased entrepreneurial activity. Because this type of growth is not likely to be inflationary, the Federal Reserve is not likely to try to counteract it. However, the speed with which decreases in taxes on income from capital lead to increases in investment is dependent on whether the Federal Reserve accomodates the increased money demand. Without accomodating monetary policy, the pace of increases in investment could be slowed, with rising interest rates creating a higher Federal debt burden. Thus, the ability to predict the actions of the Federal Reserve is important in accurately forecasting the effects of structural or supply side tax incentives.

The short-term effects of this increased investment on interest rates is further complicated by the fact that the U.S. is an open economy. To the extent that a decrease in taxes on income from capital induces an inflow of foreign financial capital, it will be necessary to predict the behavior of foreign governments in response to the corresponding outflow of financial capital from their economies. Any efforts by foreign governments to restrict these outflows could further increase U.S. interest rates.

4. Possible unintended increase in the deficit

Given the fact that most of the discussion associated with proposals to take macroeconomic effects into account has focused on proposals which are viewed, at least by some, as having the potential for positive macroeconomic effects, taking such effects into account could reduce the pressure to further reduce the deficit. Moreover, to the extent that an estimate overstates the positive macroeconomic effects of a proposed change, the result could be an increase in the deficit.

For at least the past 14 years, the CBO forecast of the deficit, and the Joint Committee forecasts of effects of tax cuts on the deficit, have been criticized by some as being too pessimistic. Yet, these forecasts have been consistently found to be too optimistic[13]. The Federal deficit increased substantially during this time. There is concern that incorporating anticipated

---

[13] In President Reagan's first budget message to Congress, it was asserted that "despite substantial rate reductions assumed in the Administration economic scenario, [it is anticipated that] Federal receipts would grow by nearly 10 percent annually...the expected $342 billion rise in Federal receipts over the 1981-1986 period is more than adequate to fund planned outlay levels..." (Americal's New Beginning: A Program for Economice Recovery, the White House, February 18, 1981, p. III-6. In fact, despite the tax increases embodied in the 1982 and 1984 tax Acts, total receipts rose by only $170 billion over the forecast period. This contributed to a total revenue shortfall of $539 billion.

growth effects would aggravate this tendency toward optimistic evaluation of fiscal policies, resulting in an additional risk of underestimating Federal deficits at a time when growing Federal debt is viewed by many as a potential long term threat to the economy.

Federal Reserve Chairman Alan Greenspan emphasized this concern in his recent testimony before a joint hearing of the House and Senate Budget Committees: "The record is very clear about one thing. This country has had no chronic problem of running smaller budget deficits (or larger surpluses) than economically desirable...It would...be a sad irony to have such long-term constructive change [as would result from a shift to consumption taxation] thwarted in practice by continuing large deficits fostered in part by unrealistic revenue estimates - estimates propelled more by perceived political needs than economic realities."[14]

---

[14] "Testimony by Alan Greenspan before a Joint Hearing of the Senate and House Committees on the Budget, January 10, 1995," pp. 9-10.

V. SUMMARY OF TESTIMONY PRESENTED TO THE JOINT HEARING OF THE HOUSE AND SENATE BUDGET COMMITTEES ON REVENUE ESTIMATING METHODOLOGY

The House and Senate Budget Committees held a joint hearing on January 10, 1995, to examine the revenue estimating process. Kenneth J. Kies, Chief of Staff of the Joint Committee on Taxation, described the current revenue estimating methodology employed by the Joint Committee staff and discussed potential changes in the methodology. Robert D. Reischauer, Director of the Congressional Budget Office (CBO), described the budget scoring process and presented the views of CBO with respect to the incorporation of behavioral effects, including their impact on macroeconomic aggregates in that process.[15]

Witnesses at the joint hearing also included Henry J. Aaron (Director of the Economic Studies Program at the Brookings Institution); Michael J. Boskin (Professor of Economics and Hoover Institution Senior Fellow, Stanford University); Martin Feldstein (President of the National Bureau of Economic Research and Professor of Economics at Harvard); Alan Greenspan (Chairman, Board of Governors of the Federal Reserve System); Rudolph G. Penner (Managing Director of Barents Group LLC, KPMG Peat Marwick, and former Director of the Congressional Budget Office); Norman B. Ture (President, Institute for Research on the Economics of Taxation); and Paul A. Volcker (Former Chairman, Board of Governors of the Federal Reserve System).

In general, these witnesses agreed that omitting the effects of tax law changes on macroeconomic aggregates such as labor supply, saving, and investment from revenue estimates may, in theory, reduce the accuracy of these estimates. Some argued that the current methodology provides biased estimates of the revenue effects of major tax proposals as a result of the omission of macroeconomic effects. However, others argued that there is no consensus on the magnitude or direction of macroeconomic effects. Some were of the opinion that the macroeconomic effects of most (if not all) tax proposals would be minimal over the five-year budget window.

There was general agreement on the principle that the inclusion of macroeconomic effects in revenue estimation methodology should be accompanied by the inclusion of such effects in estimation of the budget effects of Federal spending programs.

With the notable exception of Dr. Feldstein, the witnesses were in general agreement that there does not currently exist a well-defined methodology for incorporating macroeconomic effects into revenue estimation. Most of the witnesses urged caution in making revisions to the current estimation methodology.

The following excerpts from the written testimony of these witnesses provide a sample of their views and concerns with regard to modifications to current revenue estimating methdology.

---

[15] See Congressional Budget Office, Budget Estimates: Current Practices and Alternative Approaches, January 1995.

Henry Aaron

- "No academic consensus exists on the magnitude and often on the direction of supply-side effects of most tax changes now under consideration. And no consensus is likely to exist soon."
- "Based on all reputable estimates of the responsiveness of saving and labor supply to tax-induced changes in the rate of return, the supply-side effects of all major tax changes now under consideration could not offset (or add) more than trivially to the direct revenue effects. In short, there is not much worth fighting over."
- "Current practice is surely not quite right in ignoring aggregate demand effects, and everyone knows that it is not quite right. But I know of no responsible economist who would abandon it, because to do so would replace a faulty discipline with no discipline at all."
- "Every argument that can be put forward on behalf of including supply-side effects of tax policy in revenue estimates applies with equal or greater force to expenditure programs."

Michael Boskin

- "Static analysis of the effects of a tax proposal produces a bias in the presentation of policy choices. Tax proposals that improve economic performance are scored as losing more revenue, and sometimes far more revenue, than would be the case if dynamic estimates were used."
- "The JTC provides estimates for hundreds of tax proposals each year. Given current resources and economic knowledge, it would be impractical to develop a dynamic estimate for each of these proposals."
- "Dynamic revenue estimation should be reserved for major initiatives likely to have non-negligible effects on the economy, e.g., capital gains tax rate reduction...."
- "The dynamic estimates would require an acceptable model of the economy and/or sensible estimates of the aggregate supply responses..., what economists call elasticities. It is fair to say that there is no consensus on such a model or estimates. But that is not an excuse for doing nothing."

Martin Feldstein

- "I think the official revenue estimating method should be revised to reflect the likely effects of changes in tax rules on work and on saving."
- "[R]evenue estimators don't take into account the most important kind of economic behavior--the changes in work and saving. As a result, official projections overstate the revenue gain that would result from increasing tax rates and overstate the revenue loss that would result from lowering rates."

- "[I]t is...important to make the reforms that I am suggesting.... [T]here is nothing especially difficult about putting these reforms into practice."

Alan Greenspan

- "One central issue with respect to a more dynamic scoring is whether cyclical, aggregate demand effects of fiscal changes should be taken into account--or only permanent effects on aggregate supply. ...I would suggest that including aggregate demand effects would be confusing.... I would recommend limiting the analysis to appropriate supply-side effects."

- "[F]ully dynamic estimates of individual budget initiatives should be our goal. Unfortunately, the analytical tools required to achieve it are deficient. In fact, the goal ultimately may be unreachable. ...We should not assume that models can capture the long-run dynamic effects of specific tax and outlay changes any better than they can forecast the economy."

- "We must avoid resting key legislative decisions on controversial estimates of revenues and outlays. Should financial markets lose confidence in the integrity of our budget scoring procedures, the rise in inflation premiums and interest rates could more than offset any statistical difference between so-called static and more dynamic scoring."

Rudolph Penner

- "A significant portion of errors are made because the data with which we work is of very low quality, does not exactly fit the concepts that we require, or is outdated because it is made available with a very long time lag."

- "Even where there is more time, estimates of behavioral responses may be impractical because of...lack of data or the fact that a particular program change has never been considered in previous research."

- "[T]here is much more controversy among experts regarding the size and sometimes even the direction of the impact of policy changes on economic activity and growth than there is on micro policy issues such as the effect on the demand for gasoline from changing the gasoline tax."

- "[T]he arbitrary limit on the budget horizon is the cause of far more bad decisions than the failure to take aggregate demand and supply impacts into account."

- "The JTC and CBO should...be much more careful to explain in detail the assumptions underlying cost and revenue estimates, so that the Congress understands what is and what is not included and what biases result."

Norman Ture

- "[T]he existing methodology should be replaced by one that employs a dynamic general equilibrium model."

- "[T]he consistent application of a dynamic or general equilibrium methodology must complicate the budget-making process. Virtually every change in spending programs or in tax provisions that is made in the process of moving original budget recommendations toward budget resolution will require re-estimation of the effects on at least the major economic magnitudes, hence the feedback effects on revenues and outlays."

- The first caution...is to proceed carefully and deliberately in the development of a better estimating methodology. ...[T]here is not now available any estimating system that could be quickly adapted to the estimating needs of federal policy makers. ...[T]he Committees should not insist on undue haste that might result in adopting an unsatisfactory system that would discredit the very notion of a general equilibrium approach for estimating the budget results of public policy changes."

Paul Volcker

- "What is really at issue in the seemingly arcane matter of revenue estimating is whether...discipline will be maintained, or whether budget projections will become an act of wishful thinking...."

- "Tax changes are not unique in affecting long range productivity. An analogous case can, and certainly will, be made for certain expenditures (education, infrastructure, health and safety, on and on) spurring long-term growth, and therefore tax revenues. There simply is no possibility of reaching a strong consensus on quantifying these long-term effects...."

- "To the extent that...new estimating techniques damage both the expectations and the reality of working toward a balanced budget...the result will be higher interest rates than otherwise, reduced prospects for saving and investment, and poorer prospects for efficiency and productivity over time, not better."

Prepared Statement of William A. Niskanen

Mr. Chairman and members of the Finance Committee:

The role of numbers in policy analysis is to reduce the dispute about whether to approve a specific policy change. That role will be served only if the process for estimating the numbers is not itself subject to dispute.

The central point of my brief remarks is that any change in the process for estimating the revenue effects of tax changes should be *broadly* understood and approved—preferably by the key members of both parties in each house and by the administration. Such a change should be considered the equivalent of a change in the bylaws of a club or a change in the scoring rules in an athletic league. Such changes should be approved only by the support of most of the affected groups, not by only those who expect to benefit most from the change in the short term.

Some other comparisons may help illustrate the issues bearing on the choice between static and dynamic revenue estimates:

- Static estimating is an application of arithmetic. Many politicians are not very good at arithmetic, but it does not evoke much partisan dispute. Dynamic estimating is based on some model of economic behavior, a model that reflects some theory of how people behave and estimates of how they respond to specific types of changes in the conditions they face. Some of the characteristic differences between parties involve differences on just these issues.
- In that case, static estimating is somewhat like democracy—it may be the best deal we can make with our neighbors.

But we should try to convince our neighbors if there is reason we can do better. And dynamic estimates can be much more accurate than static estimates. In general, people will do more of some activity if the after-tax returns are increased and less of this activity if after-tax returns are reduced, and that is the basis for the higher potential accuracy of the dynamic estimates. We would probably make better tax policy decisions even on the basis of crude dynamic assumptions—for example, that tax increases increase revenue and that tax reductions reduce revenue by only half that estimated by static models.

But we should be able to make even more accurate estimates. There are still some differences in the estimates of the magnitude and timing of the responses to tax changes, but some of these differences can be resolved by focusing on the same scope of responses. For prime age males, for example, the response of hours worked to a change in after-tax wages appears to be close to zero; the effect of tax rates on taxable earnings, however, is higher, reflecting the response of taxable earnings to tax-induced effects on occupation, location, and tax avoidance. Similarly, the response of the savings rate to the after-tax interest rate appears to be close to zero; the effect of tax rates on taxable interest payments, however, is higher, reflecting the tax-induced effect on the type of investment. The full behavioral response to change in taxes is often substantially higher than the first stage response, especially in the long run.

May I suggest, however, that the revenue estimators stop short of including the potential demand-side effects of tax changes. First, there continues to be a major disagreement among macroeconomists as to whether tax changes have any significant effect on aggregate demand. (On that issue, my position is that most changes in fiscal policy have no significant effect on aggregate demand, but I acknowledge that many of my professional colleagues believe otherwise.) And second, any demand-side effects can be offset by changes in monetary policy. For these reasons, I suggest, estimates of the dynamic effects of tax changes on tax revenues should be based on supply-side models, not on the older form of Keynesian macromodels.

The next steps toward making sense of this issue, I suggest, are the following:

- First, put to rest the wholly false, albeit common, charge that the unexpected increases in the federal deficit in the early 1980s were due to misleading dynamic supply-side revenue forecasts. In fact, all of the budget forecasts by both the administration and Congress were based on static revenue estimates; moreover, the OMB and CBO budget forecasts in 1981 were remarkably similar. The federal deficits of the early 1980s proved to be substantially higher than expected for several reasons—the unusually deep recession of 1981–1982, a faster-than-expected decline in inflation, and a failure to maintain spending restraint beyond the first Reagan budget. All of the budget forecasts during this period substantially underestimated the deficit, but not because they were based on supply-side models.
- Second, those who favor higher taxes should acknowledge that increases in the top marginal income tax rates generate little increased revenue; a given increase in tax rates at this level is a larger proportionate reduction in the after-tax rate, and high income taxpayers have more opportunities for legal tax avoid-

ance. Similarly, those who favor lower taxes should acknowledge that some tax cuts reduce revenues by more than the state estimates. The $500 tax credit for children proposed in the House Republican Contract, for example, would generate larger dynamic revenue losses to the extent that it increases birth rates or reduces the participation of women in the paid labor force. These examples illustrate that dynamic revenue forecasts do not necessarily favor the preferred policies of either party.

- Third, the Joint Committee on Taxation should open up its estimating methods and invite peer review. May I suggest that you start this process by asking the respected National Bureau of Economic Research to sponsor studies and a conference on the JCT methodology and on the most important next steps to improve the revenue forecasts. Leading public finance economists should be asked to comment on the JCT methodology and report to Congress, maybe at hearings before this committee, on their evaluations and recommendations.
- And finally, pending completion of this review, no change in the JCT methodology is appropriate. A substantial consensus among leading public finance economists, I suggest, is probably necessary to broaden the support for proposed changes to this methodology across parties in Congress and with the administration. And, as I introduced my testimony, more accurate revenue forecasts from the best possible dynamic model would help resolve differences on tax policy only if the methodology by which the forecasts are generated is endorsed by most of the major participants in the policy debate.

Thank you.

○

88-270(92)

